ON THE WATERFRONT

....

Leo Braudy

bfi Publishing

First published in 2005 by the
BRITISH FILM INSTITUTE
21 Stephen Street, London W1T 1LN

The British Film Institute's purpose is to
champion moving image culture in all its richness
and diversity across the UK, for the benefit
of as wide an audience as possible,
and to create debate.

British Library Cataloguing-in-Publication Data
A catalogue record for this book is available from the British Library

ISBN 1–84457–072–X

Series design by
Andrew Barron & Collis Clements Associates

Typeset in Fournier and Franklin Gothic by
D R Bungay Associates, Burghfield, Berks

Printed in the UK by
Cromwell Press, Trowbridge, Wiltshire

CONTENTS

ON THE WATERFRONT

In 1955 *On the Waterfront* became one of the most honoured films at any Oscar ceremony. But unlike such spectacles as *An American in Paris* (1951), *The Greatest Show on Earth* (1952), *Around the World in Eighty Days* (1956) and *Ben-Hur* (1959), which also received Oscars, *On the Waterfront* was a work of gritty realism, more indebted to the look of Italian neo-realist films like *Rome Open City* (1945) and *Bicycle Thieves* (1947) than to the widescreen Technicolor extravaganzas of the studios. Produced by the maverick Sam Spiegel on a comparative shoestring, the film was at first what Elia Kazan, the director, and Budd Schulberg, the scriptwriter, called an 'orphan', turned down by every major studio, then grudgingly financed, shot on location along the Hoboken, New Jersey, docks across the Hudson river from New York City, and taking for its story working-class problems in a working-class neighbourhood.

Nevertheless, *On the Waterfront* received nine awards including Best Film, equalling the record of *From Here to Eternity* the previous year and *Gone With the Wind* nineteen years before. In addition, Kazan received the Oscar for Best Director (his second), while acting awards went to Marlon Brando and Eva Marie Saint, Best Story and Screenplay to Schulberg, Best Editing (Gene Milford), Best Black-and-White Cinematography (Boris Kaufman) and Best Black-and-White Set Decoration (Richard Day). Its Academy-Award-nominated music was written by Leonard Bernstein, his only original movie score.

On the Waterfront has endured as both a popular film and a classic while many of the more grandiose films of the period have disappeared from cultural memory. The incessantly repeated images of its taxicab confrontation between Brando and Rod Steiger have made the film iconic to huge audiences that may have never seen it in its entirety. With that scene, as well as the getting-to-know-you interchange between Brando and Saint over her glove, and the nominations of Karl Malden, Lee J. Cobb and Steiger for acting Oscars as well, *On the Waterfront* also solidified the reputation of the Actors Studio as a training ground for a new generation of American actors and familiarised audiences with the 'Method' – an acting style that emphasised psychological realism rather than the more declamatory methods taught in British acting schools. As Christina Pickles, then a student at the Royal Academy of Dramatic Arts (RADA), remembers it:

We cut Rapid Diction class to go see the film. It was a revelation. We immediately went back to an empty classroom, where Brian Bedford and I tried to improvise a scene. We had never done that kind of thing before and we had certainly never been taught it.

Dealing with corruption on the New York–New Jersey docks, *On the Waterfront* was also a social problem film of a sort that seemed to have become outmoded in the golden sun of 50s' American prosperity. Yet at the same time it was severely criticised by the left in America (and England) for what they considered to be its vindication of informing, when the hero Terry Malloy finally decides to testify against the corrupt union leader. This was a volatile issue because Kazan, Schulberg and co-star Lee J. Cobb had all testified as friendly witnesses to the House UnAmerican Activities Committee (HUAC), naming names of former Communist associates. Upset by Kazan's testimony, Brando, whose career had been launched by Kazan in *A Streetcar Named Desire*, twice returned the script unread, until the producer Sam Spiegel persuaded him to take the part.

On the Waterfront thus has an important place in the careers of Kazan and Brando, two of the most significant figures in American film and theatre of the 1950s. Its showcasing of Method acting had a tremendous influence on both American and European performance styles as well as plots. Its political issues and the controversies around its production mirror the conflicts of the Cold War and the anti-Communist paranoia gripping the United States.

Yet the complexities of the film belie any easy equation between the political beliefs of its creators, the actions of its characters and the shape of its plot. Within the film itself is a kind of ambivalence about moral behaviour (figured visually in the constant mists of the Hoboken waterfront) and the difficulty of moral choices that gives it a resonance beyond the partisan politics of its day.

Like so many heroes of the period – J. D. Salinger's Holden Caulfield, Jack Kerouac's Sal Paradise and Dean Moriarty, or the characters played by James Dean and Montgomery Clift in a variety of movies – Brando's Terry Malloy is a young man trying to find out how to grow up. This is another chord that *On the Waterfront* strikes in the post-war world – the appeal of the anti-hero. He is not the traditional hero whose easy choices and actions make the world whole but a newer sort of protagonist whose actions illustrate the difficulty of maintaining one's identity and integrity amid the world's incoherence. Instead of neatly tying up all conflicts in a balanced resolution, the end of *On the Waterfront*, so notoriously attacked in Lindsay Anderson's *Sight and Sound* essay soon after it appeared, leaves its issues unresolved and still disturbing.

In fact, it is tempting to argue that naming names before the HUAC put Kazan into a moral and psychological quandary that paradoxically made him a better director. Comparing the moral questions – and the visual style – of his previous Oscar-winning film *Gentleman's Agreement* (1947) with *On the Waterfront* is instructive. *Gentleman's Agreement* is all evenly lit moral clarity: anti-Semitism is wrong; Gregory Peck is our reporter–hero for exposing it by pretending he is Jewish, although he is never really in jeopardy himself. *On The Waterfront* is much more ambivalent: Terry Malloy seems to move from the corrupt world of the gang of union thugs to the moral high ground of testifying about Joey Doyle's murder. But at the end, a bloody and beaten symbol of resistance to the mob, he is as much manipulated by Karl Malden's Father Barry as he had been by his brother Charley and gang boss Johnny Friendly. In his own preliminary notes about the character, Kazan identifies Terry's mixture of shame and bravado with his own compound of immigrant striving and energy, coupled with a resentment about his efforts to be ingratiating before his testimony alienated him from old associates and friends: 'Yourself during *Waiting for Lefty* – or when you were the white-haired boy-director. With what pride you used to walk around! – with what confidence!! … He's the last person the mob would expect to have any trouble with.' As Kazan often remarks to himself in these notes, despite his undergraduate study at Williams, the prestigious New England liberal arts college, despite his time in the Group Theatre, one of the most celebrated and influential theatre companies of the 1930s, and despite his resounding successes in both film and theatre, he still felt perpetually outside, a position that his HUAC testimony had only confirmed. 'I despised my nickname … Gadget! It suggested an agreeable, ever-compliant little cuss, a "good Joe" who worked hard and always followed instructions. I didn't feel that way, not at all.'[1]

The Lure of the Waterfront

Born in Istanbul in 1909, Kazan emigrated to the United States with his family in 1913. After attending Williams College and Yale Drama School, he joined the embryonic Group Theatre, one of the many amateur and professional leftwing groups of the 1930s. It was destined to become the most influential because of its intense commitment not only to political content but also to elaborating for American performers the theories of acting developed by Constantin Stanislavsky for the Moscow Art Theatre.

At first an actor and assistant stage manager, Kazan continued to act in theatre and films up till and through 1941, but gradually concentrated more of his energies on direction. In 1942 he had a great success on Broadway with Thornton Wilder's *The Skin of Our Teeth* and in 1945 directed his first film *A Tree Grows in Brooklyn*, for which two of the actors, James Dunn and Peggy Ann Garner, received Academy Awards.

Kazan was building an enviable reputation not only as a director with a special sensitivity to acting but also one who worked closely with playwrights. In 1947, along with Robert Lewis and Cheryl Crawford, who had been fellow members of the Group Theatre, he co-founded the Actors Studio to furnish a place where American actors could work on their craft. 1947 was also a big year for Kazan professionally. On stage he directed Arthur Miller's *All My Sons* and Tennessee Williams's *A Streetcar Named Desire*. On film, he directed *Sea of Grass*, *Boomerang!*, and *Gentleman's Agreement*. *Streetcar* received the Pulitzer Prize and Kazan won the directing Academy Award for *Gentleman's Agreement*. The next year on Broadway he directed Lee J. Cobb in Miller's *Death of a Salesman*, which also received the Pulitzer Prize.

Death of a Salesman, Mildred Dunnock, Arthur Kennedy, Lee J. Cobb as Willy Loman (speaking), and Cameron Mitchell

Elia Kazan on the set of *Baby Doll* (1956)

Kazan, Brando, Julie Harris, and James Dean on the set of *East of Eden* (1955)

Meanwhile, in late 1947 Arthur Miller was frequenting the Red Hook section of Brooklyn doing research for a script that would deal with crime and corruption on the waterfront. As he tells the story in his autobiography *Timebends*, he had been inspired by the tales of a rebel leader named Pete Panto who had battled the gang-run unions. Panto was a young union activist who had been murdered in 1939 but whose name was still written in graffiti on neighbourhood walls: *Dov'é Pete Panto? Where is Pete Panto?* 'The idea of a young man defying evil and ending in a cement block at the bottom of the river drew me on.'[2]

Since Kazan was looking for a film project as well, he and Miller decided to work together. But when the script, now called *The Hook*, was finished and they went out to Hollywood in 1951 to try to sell it to Columbia, they met a stone wall.[3] HUAC had held hearings in Hollywood in 1947, issuing subpoenas to forty-three members of the Hollywood community. A group dubbed the 'unfriendly 19' chose not to co-operate with HUAC on First Amendment grounds. Of these nineteen, ten were finally cited for contempt of Congress. This group, known as the Hollywood Ten, included writers Ring Lardner, Jr, John Howard Lawson, Dalton Trumbo, and Albert Maltz, directors Herbert Biberman and Edward Dmytryk, and actor Larry Parks. Meanwhile, another group, including the directors John Huston and William Wyler, the actors Humphrey Bogart and Fredric March and the writer Philip Dunne, formed a Committee for the First Amendment as a liberal response to HUAC.

Threatened politically by HUAC and financially by government anti-trust suits and the rising popularity of television, Hollywood executives were running scared. At the Waldorf Conference later that year, a majority of the studios declared they would not hire anyone who had not 'purged' his Communist past, creating a de facto 'blacklist'.

In the ensuing years blacklisting spread in the entertainment industry, the Ten were sent to jail and fined when the Supreme Court refused to hear their appeal, and in 1951 HUAC was back in Hollywood. More 'friendly' witnesses testified, while many blacklisted directors, producers, and scriptwriters, including Joseph Losey, Carl Foreman and Jules Dassin, moved abroad in search of work.

Darryl Zanuck at Fox had already turned the Miller script down and was more interested in the Steinbeck–Kazan project *Viva Zapata!* (1952). Warners had also passed and, in this atmosphere, Harry Cohn, the head of Columbia, told Miller and Kazan that, even though he liked the script, he would do it only with FBI approval. The fount of that approval was Roy

Brewer, the head of the International Alliance of Theatrical State Employees (IATSE), the parent organisation of the film craft unions, and the person who had become the final court of appeal for anyone in Hollywood who wanted to purge a radical past and get off the blacklist. According to *Timebends*, Miller was back in New York when Kazan called to tell him that Brewer had told Cohn that the script was all a lie, that there was no gangster influence on the waterfront, and the union revolt should be against Communist leaders, not mobsters. In Kazan's account, both he and Miller as well as Cohn are present at the meeting where Brewer says that despite what Miller had written about corruption in the waterfront unions, gangsters were much less of a problem than Communists, and the hero should at some point explicitly reject their support. Miller is silent, while Kazan temporises by saying they would talk later about what kind of revisions to make. 'We felt humiliated, so much so that we couldn't discuss the problem.'[4] Miller then leaves for the East Coast, while Kazan goes to a budget meeting that implies to him that Cohn is still willing to do the picture. In Kazan's account, Miller sends some revisions, and Kazan is set to ensure Columbia commits enough money to the project so that Cohn cannot easily back out. But in the middle of the budget meeting, he gets a phone call from Miller to say he is withdrawing the script. In Miller's account, he never makes any revisions and returns to New York to find a telegram from Cohn: 'ITS INTERESTING HOW THE MINUTE WE TRY TO MAKE THE SCRIPT PRO-AMERICAN YOU PULL OUT. HARRY COHN.' Kazan for his part continues to wonder why Miller withdrew *The Hook* when things were actually looking up for the potential film. 'What was Art protecting – his script or himself? ... I didn't believe he'd been a Communist; he knew I had. Even though we were close friends, we had never discussed the matter.'[5]

Kazan goes on to speculate whether troubles in Miller's personal life might have been a cause – his failing marriage and his blossoming love for Marilyn Monroe, whom they had both met while in Hollywood for meetings about *The Hook*, and with whom Kazan quickly began an affair. But he never finds out why, and the disparities between his account of the death of *The Hook* and Miller's raise more questions than they resolve. Martin Gottfried in his biography of Miller seems to accept the personal explanation, that Miller's abrupt departure from Hollywood was 'a flight from his own freshly uncovered and terrifying (because compelling) sexuality'; at other moments in his book, however, he mentions Miller's vagueness whenever pressed about his political affiliations. Appropriately enough, Miller goes on to write *The Crucible*

(1953), with its clear analogies between the Salem witch trials and paranoia about Communism. Both there and in *A View from the Bridge* (1955), informing is a central issue, although in the later play the informer is viewed more sympathetically. No wonder perhaps that John Proctor in *The Crucible* assuages his sexual guilt by his political refusal to incriminate others.[6]

Meanwhile, Budd Schulberg had himself been writing about the New York waterfront for some time, although the exact story that would finally become the film was still a long way off. There, Terry Malloy, an ex-boxer and longshoreman, is the younger brother of Charley, the 'brains' of a mob running a corrupt union led by Johnny Friendly. When Joey Doyle, a longshoreman about to testify to the Waterfront Crime Commission, is murdered with Terry's collusion, Joey's sister Edie sets out on a crusade to discover his killer. Father Barry, a priest in a local church, is also turned into an activist by Joey's death and by Edie's sarcasm about his detachment from the lives his parishioners lead. When Terry helps Edie escape from a gang attack on a meeting Father Barry is leading, a relationship begins to build between them, which plays on Terry's sense of guilt over Joey's murder, even though Terry is still loyal to Charley and Johnny Friendly. Meanwhile another longshoreman, 'Kayo' Dugan, agrees to testify.

Terry also receives a subpoena, but to Edie's disgust, tears it up. After Dugan is murdered in front of Terry and other longshoremen unloading a ship, Terry goes to Father Barry to confess his involvement in Joey's murder. Barry persuades Terry to tell Edie and she runs off horrified. Meanwhile the gang has found out about Terry's subpoena and Charley is delegated to make sure he will not testify. In the famous taxicab scene between Charley and Terry, Terry realises how often his own dreams have been thwarted by Charley and Johnny and implies that he might testify after all. Later, while he is attempting to reconcile with Edie after his confession, a cry from the street says that Charley is looking for him. Narrowly escaping from a truck bent on running them down, he and Edie discover Charley's body hung on a wall by a longshoreman's hook. Terry goes to Johnny's bar to seek revenge, but is persuaded by Father Barry to testify publicly instead. After the testimony, Terry is shunned by the other longshoremen. He goes to the gang clubhouse by the river to fight with Johnny Friendly and finish what he started. Beaten bloody from the fight, Terry nevertheless leads the other longshoremen into work, despite Johnny's threats.

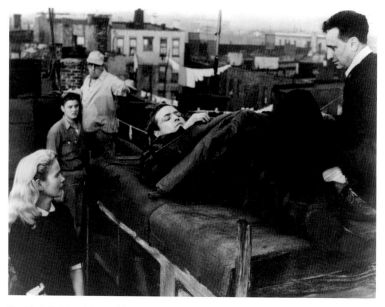

Eva Marie Saint watches as Kazan directs Brando on top of the pigeon loft

14   Brando and Saint sitting on a pier in the Hudson River before (or after) the scene in which
Terry Malloy confesses to Edie Doyle he set up her brother to be murdered

This in broad outline is the final story of *On the Waterfront*. But the path to it was hardly so direct. In fact, there were some eight versions along the way and their evolution indicates some intriguing differences between the ways Schulberg and Kazan conceived the film.[7]

Like Miller on the Brooklyn waterfront a few years before, Schulberg had become fascinated with the brutal conflict taking place only a few blocks away from Manhattan's glittering skyscrapers. In 1949 he had been asked by Joseph Curtis, a nephew of Harry Cohn's, to write a script based on Malcolm Johnson's series of New York *Sun* articles 'Crime on the Waterfront', which began appearing the day before the 1948 strike and in book form would receive the Pulitzer Prize for Journalism in 1950.[8] Aside from work on several forgettable films of the late 1930s and early 1940s, Schulberg, the son of B. P. Schulberg, one of the founders of Hollywood and the longtime head of production at Paramount, had devoted most of his attention to fiction. His satiric Hollywood novel *What Makes Sammy Run?* appeared in 1941, when he was a precocious twenty-seven. During the war he worked for the Office of Strategic Services (OSS) and was later in charge of gathering visual images for the Nuremberg trials, where his duties included serving a subpoena on Leni Riefenstahl. By his own account, having witnessed the disregard in which scriptwriters were held in Hollywood, Schulberg thought he would never write a film script again.[9] In 1947 he published *The Harder They Fall*, a prize-fighting novel loosely based on the career of Primo Carnero that exposed the manipulations of crooked fight managers. In 1950 came *The Disenchanted*, drawn from his experiences accompanying F. Scott Fitzgerald to Dartmouth to write the film *Winter Carnival* (1939).

Malcolm Johnson sent Schulberg for first-hand information to Father John Corridan, the associate director of the Xavier Institute of Industrial Relations on Manhattan's Lower West Side, a Jesuit-run American version of the 'worker–priest' movement in South America set up in the wake of Pius XI's *Quadragesimo anno* encyclical of 1931, which criticised both capitalism and socialism.[10] After he gained Father Corridan's confidence as being more than just a sightseer ('At first he was rather sarcastic about me'), Schulberg was introduced to longshoremen who had been fighting the corrupt rule of Joseph Ryan, the head of the International Longshoremen's Association (ILA), as well as to the array of thugs and gangsters who filled so many union posts. Schulberg's chief guide among the 'insoigents' was the feisty Arthur Brown, who had survived several attacks by ILA mobsters. 'Brownie' and his colourful language later made an indelible mark on Schulberg's scripts. He became the model for a series of characters that finally coalesced in 'Kayo' Dugan, the longshoreman who testifies and is then murdered. Brown also worked on the film itself, building the pigeon coop and appearing in some group scenes.[11]

Moved by Corridan's commitment to the dockers and his charismatic personality, Schulberg began working on his script and writing articles about the waterfront situation. By early 1951, the *New York Times* noted that Schulberg was at work on the script with Robert Siodmak, who had been signed as director by Curtis's Monticello Film Corporation, which owned the rights to Johnson's work. Siodmak, like Kazan later, wanted to use New York actors for the film and commented that 'We will try to avoid plot as much as possible and make the most use of characterisation and the wonderful waterfront backgrounds.'[12] This early script focuses not on a Terry Malloy figure but on a reporter who starts investigating the waterfront and runs into similar trouble with the gangs. That central character was revived some decades later when Schulberg wrote a stage version of *On the Waterfront*.

From the very start of his various versions of the scripts, Schulberg therefore focuses more on Father Barry than he does on Terry Malloy. In the earliest versions, Terry is only one among several characters. In the script titled *Bottom of the River*, for example, it is Terry, not 'Kayo' Dugan, who is killed by the falling sling and it is a reporter named Chase who forms an alliance with Edie and the priest, then the central characters. In another earlier version, entitled *Crime on the Waterfront*, the main characters again include the reporter Chase, Father Moran and Edie, here Terry's sister. When Terry (called Terry Monahan in this version) disappears midway through the story, Edie enlists the priest and the reluctant reporter to try to find him.

By the time of the version called *The Golden Warriors*, which would be the name for the script until it became *On the Waterfront*, the reporter has dropped out and Terry has become more prominent, although the story is still far from what the film will be. This Terry is a coarse and even vulgar character who tries to put the moves on Edie, no longer his sister. This more sexual atmosphere is helped along by the character of May, Edie's sister, a stereotypical 'loose woman'. In this version as well, Edie is more active, accepting a date with Terry's brother Charley at a fancy restaurant and going to a party at the apartment of Mr Big, where she is discovered rifling through the files on his desk looking for evidence that would help her solve Joey's murder. This Edie-asdetective plot turn is heavily criticised by Darryl Zanuck in a long memo to Schulberg and Kazan in February 1953.

In later versions, middle-level characters like Edie's slutty sister May and her Uncle Frank, an honest cop, are pared away to concentrate on the central figures. Similarly, the locations are concentrated as well. A scene at a fight where Terry shows Edie how he takes a fall is gone, as is the scene of the improbable Edie–Charley date and the party at Mr Big's Manhattan apartment. All these changes create a greater economy in the unfolding of the story that moves the centre of gravity in Schulberg's script away from Father Barry's moral dilemmas about both his own activism and his encouragement of the longshoremen to testify, and towards the inner turmoil of Terry Malloy. Not coincidentally, it was exactly the shift that Zanuck had recommended in his memos and one affirmed by notes Kazan took down from both Sam Spiegel and Robert Ardrey, a playwright with whom Kazan had worked in the Group Theatre and the mentor of Karl Malden.

Although Schulberg had extensively researched and written about the waterfront, including several articles for the *New York Times Magazine* and his own work on the early scripts was exactly contemporary with that of Kazan and Miller, some critics have persistently claimed that *On the Waterfront* is in some way a partial ripoff, if not an outright plagiarism, of the script for *The Hook*.[13] One moment in particular that is frequently cited is the scene where the hiring boss throws the work tabs in the air and the longshoremen fight to pick one up to get a day's work. This occurs at the shape-up, the notorious feature of waterfront hiring that is a prime focus of all the labour agitation of the period. Kazan, who was also taken around the Brooklyn waterfront when Miller was working on the script, may have witnessed such a scene.[14] In any case, the situation is very different in the two plots. In *The Hook* it is a nervous clerk, sitting in for the hiring boss, who throws two paper tabs in the air and there is nothing of the various secret gestures that guarantee a longshoreman work; in *On the Waterfront*, by contrast, it is the brutal Big Mac who gleefully throws the tabs to humiliate the longshoremen. 'Meatballs', says one of the mobsters. 'Definitely', says the other.

Aside from a few scenes like this that take place because both scripts deal with the waterfront and longshoremen, they have little in common in either plot or atmosphere. *The Hook*, with its focus on meetings and family conclaves, is reminiscent of the agit-prop plays of the 1930s. Unlike *On the Waterfront* as either script(s) or film, there is little detail in *The Hook* of daily life on the docks: the kickbacks, the loansharking, the daily despair of the shape-up. The focus instead is almost entirely on the corrupt union situation and the efforts of Marty Ferrara, the central character, to change it by organising his fellow workers. As a radical unionist, Ferrara is a very different kind of hero from Terry Malloy. He has a wife and family, who are put in jeopardy by his actions, while Terry is an alienated loner, whose only supports are his brother and the gang, and whose only pleasure and time of ease come from going on the tenement roof to raise and race his pigeons. Whereas there are family meals and children in *The Hook*, we never see Terry's apartment in *On the Waterfront* and the only children apparent are the mobster-wannabes of the Golden Warriors.[15] Despite the brief scenes in Pop Doyle's apartment, there is a sense of drifting and uprootedness that permeates the film. All in all, life in *On the Waterfront* is a much lonelier experience than life in *The Hook*, and the politics of the film, the ins and outs of union manoeuvring that fascinate Miller in *The Hook*, have vanished and in their place are more psychological themes.

Despite the coincidence of two waterfront scripts being developed at the same time, it seems no accident that Miller, Schulberg and Kazan, who had all grown up during the 1930s' celebration of radical politics and especially trade unionism, should be drawn to what was one of the most widespread union conflicts of the post-war period. World War II had for the most part repressed union agitation in the name of patriotism. But in 1945, 1948 and 1951 there were extensive wildcat strikes on the New York–New Jersey waterfront specifically attacking sweetheart contracts signed by the leaders of the ILA with the ship owners. All the 1930s faith that trade unionism could change the face of American capitalism was being tested by this world where unions had secret agreements with employers, where gangsters kept the rank and file in line, and where men who dared to speak out were in danger of their lives.[16]

Miller had been introduced to the Brooklyn waterfront by Vincent James Longhi, a lawyer, and Mitch Berenson, a longshoreman, both associated with the American Labor Party. As a result, much of *The Hook* is shaped by what they showed him and their own attitude to waterfront politics. Miller's preoccupation with Pete Panto also recalls Clifford Odets's play *Waiting for Lefty*, in which a strike is called by taxi drivers inspired by the murder of Lefty, their rebel leader. Kazan had played a small but significant role when it was produced by the Group Theatre in 1935, beginning the famous 'Strike!' chant that ends the play.

By contrast, Father Corridan had been Schulberg's guide into the waterfront world and he remains the centre of Schulberg's interest, even as the script develops into a greater exploration of Terry's character. Corridan's 1948 speech about the waterfront ('Christ is in the shape-up'), which Schulberg quotes extensively in Father Barry's crucifixion speech after the murder of 'Kayo' Dugan, already infuses the early scripts with images of sacrifice and redemption. The successful fusion of these very different visions of the meaning of the story of *On the Waterfront* would later be characterised by Kazan as 'a series of accidents and misfortunes that turned out well in the end'.[17]

In December 1952, just a month before Arthur Miller's *The Crucible* opened on Broadway, Schulberg bought the rights to Johnson's articles from Monticello, which had been unable to get backers for the film. The project was now being called *Bottom of the River*. In the meantime Kazan became interested as well. Puzzled by Arthur Miller's withdrawal of *The Hook* from consideration by Harry Cohn at Columbia, Kazan still wanted to make a film on the East Coast with a social and political theme. He had never met Schulberg, but admired him for quitting the Communist Party after refusing to make changes in *What Makes Sammy Run?* when pressured by Party cultural commissars. Once Kazan's testimony was made public, Schulberg wrote him a letter of sympathy for the vilification he was undergoing, and Kazan got in touch with him about possibly working together. At first they toyed with the idea of a film about the Trenton Six, a group of black teenagers who had been convicted in 1948 of murdering a white shopkeeper. The case had become a cause célèbre for radicals in New York and New Jersey, reminiscent of the Scottsboro Boys case from the 1930s which had fascinated Schulberg as a teenager.[18]

Then, when Schulberg mentioned his waterfront script and Kazan said that he also had a waterfront project that had fallen through, the partnership seemed inevitable. But Schulberg was still wary because of his Hollywood experience as a writer who had been shunted aside once the script was finished. Kazan in turn promised to treat his work just as he had treated Williams and Miller. As Schulberg later remarked, 'I don't think any director from that time to this has treated a screenwriter with that kind of respect. He spoiled me.' In her book on the collaboration between Kazan and Tennessee Williams, Brenda Murphy argues that Kazan had in fact helped pioneer on Broadway this way of working with writers, on the model of the Group Theatre's effort to include the playwright in the creative process of production. The norm in the 1930s and into the 1940s had been that the playwright would furnish the text and then disappear, leaving the rest to the director and the producer. But with Williams and Miller, Kazan was involved in the project from the start and

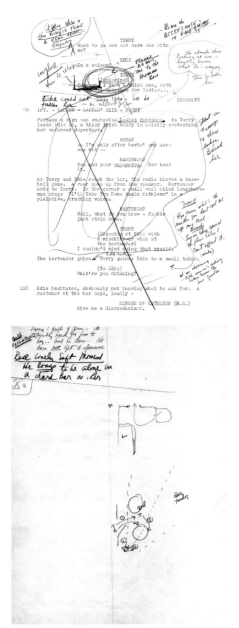

Pages from Kazan's copy of the script, with his dialogue rewritings, notes, and drawings of camera angles for the bar scene with Edie and Terry

in his turn involved the playwright in the production. As even a cursory scrutiny of the scripts in the archive of his career housed at Wesleyan University reveals, Kazan was constantly annotating, questioning and revising Schulberg's drafts, as well as making notes for himself about possible camera movements and the order of shots, how lines should be read, which bits of dialogue should be done quickly, which swallowed and which said more loudly. Interleaved are also relevant newspaper articles, photographs that suggest setups, and comments on the characters and actions.

Recent events had associated Schulberg and Kazan in other ways as well. In May 1951, Schulberg had testified to HUAC about his trip to Russia in 1934 to attend the Congress of Soviet Writers, his 1936–40 membership in the Communist Party and the controversy over *What Makes Sammy Run?* that caused him to break with the Party. In January 1952, Kazan had refused to testify about anyone but himself to the Committee, but in April, after telling Clifford Odets and Paula Strasberg what he was going to do, he named them along with six other members of the Group Theatre and several Party functionaries. A day after his testimony was released to the press, an advertisement in his name, but written by his wife Molly Day Thacher, was printed in the *New York Times*. In the name of saying 'Liberals must speak out', Kazan justified his testimony and attacked Communists for the 'pretense that they stand for the very things which they kill in their own countries ... free speech, a free press, the rights of property, the rights of labor, racial equality and, above all, individual rights'. [19]

Perhaps even more than his testimony, this advertisement made Kazan a lightning rod for all the understandable hostility from both the Communist and the anti-Communist left about what HUAC's witch hunt and the blacklist had done to show business. Many had testified and many more would, some even of similar stature. But Kazan then, and until his death almost fifty years later, bore the brunt of resentment – both from those who reasonably resented what he had done and from those for whom condemning Kazan was a badge of political and moral purity. Responding to Schulberg's sympathetic letter in the midst of widespread hostility from so many of his former friends and associates (including Arthur Miller), Kazan and his wife travelled to Schulberg's farm in Pennsylvania for a visit. This almost happenstance meeting, which would ultimately produce a great film, also planted the seeds of later accusations that *On the Waterfront* was designed to justify informing, charges which Kazan often embraced and Schulberg consistently denied. [20]

But such criticisms were all in the future and I will deal with their relation to the film later. A few points deserve mention now, however. In the wake of Cohn's rejection of *The Hook*, specifically citing Miller's refusal to make the gangsters Communists, Kazan may have felt the hot breath of HUAC on his back. At virtually the same time that he was testifying, he was also publicly defending *Viva Zapata!* against criticisms that focused on the character of Fernando, a strangely mannered political robot who constantly changes sides depending on where the power is.[21] After *Zapata* and before *Waterfront*, he also made *Man on a Tightrope*, a film about an East German circus whose owner (Fredric March) plans a daring escape into West Germany for the entire troupe. Shot in a sun- and rain-drenched style that recalls Jean Renoir's *Partie de campagne* (1936), *Man on a Tightrope*, although based on a true story, has the atmosphere of a Cold War fable. It had been proposed to Kazan by Darryl Zanuck as a way of quieting those on the right who thought that Kazan was still politically suspect despite his testimony. Zanuck had already told Kazan that he was too controversial and his salary would be cut accordingly. At first Kazan refused to make the film, but then finally agreed, bringing on board March, another blacklisted actor, as well as Adolphe Menjou, who had been a friendly witness: 'It turned out that Menjou was no more a Fascist threat than Freddie was a Communist.'[22]

Whatever their hostility to the Party itself, both Kazan and Schulberg seemed to continue to think of themselves as political and social radicals, perhaps even more so after their testimonies. Kazan's desire to make an 'Eastern' dealing with a social problem, like Schulberg's immersion in the conflicts down at the Manhattan waterfront, have the air of an effort to return to those concerns that had animated their politics, and their art, from the beginning. Almost forty years later, in his autobiography, Kazan was even more explicit:

> I was more determined than ever to make a film about the New York harbor and what went on there, thus to show everyone, including myself, that I hadn't backed away from my convictions and wasn't to be insulted or bullied again.[23]

How successful they would be in making such a film was another question. Kazan still contractually owed 20th Century-Fox a film and he decided that it would be *On the Waterfront*. The prospects seemed good because Fox had negotiated with Joseph Curtis for the project as early as 1949. Schulberg finished the script while continuing to write journalistic pieces about the waterfront for magazines and newspapers. But when they boarded the Super Chief for the four-day train ride to Los Angeles, even though Kazan was full of enthusiasm, Schulberg was beginning to have doubts about their chances. He had not worked in Hollywood for years, while Kazan had recently made two films, one controversial (*Viva Zapata!*) and the other a popular and critical flop (*Man on a Tightrope*). In addition, both had been attacked by a hostile left and a suspicious right. What kind of welcome could they expect from Zanuck?

As it turned out, Schulberg's cynicism was more prophetic than Kazan's exuberance. No limo waited for them at the train station, no flowers were in their room at the Beverly Hills Hotel, and when they finally got to Zanuck's office, they had to wait in line behind Bella Darvi, a new mistress Zanuck was promoting as a starlet. Once in the office, Zanuck wasted no time in letting them know where he thought the industry was going, and it wasn't in the direction of a black-and-white film about dockworkers. Technicolor, CinemaScope, Cinerama, he gushed, and asked them what they thought of his new project, *Prince Valiant* (1954), based on a popular comic strip.

Political pressure may have been in the background, but Zanuck was also going where the money and the audiences were. In 1953, with such Fox films as *The Robe* (Henry Koster), the first to be released in CinemaScope, and *How to Marry a Millionaire* (Jean Negulesco) with Marilyn Monroe, colour and widescreen had brought a new fascination with historical spectacle and an inundation of glossy and gleaming consumer goods. Black and white by the same token was coming to signify a lower-class setting as well as a more artsy, even 'foreign' perspective.

Finally, when Kazan forced the *Waterfront* issue, Zanuck responded. Despite having written extensive memos to them, detailing his enthusiasm for the story even while he criticised certain aspects of the plot and asked for rewrites, Zanuck had now somehow turned against the project. Not only did he not like the script, he said, he hated the whole idea. Kazan's rosy vision of the socially conscious Zanuck who made *Young Mr. Lincoln* (1939), *The Grapes of Wrath* (1940), *Gentleman's Agreement* and *Viva Zapata!* vanished. 'Who's going to care about a lot of sweaty longshoremen?' Zanuck roared, and proceeded to denounce Kazan for bringing him projects like *Zapata* and this one: 'I think what you've written is exactly what the American people don't want to see.'[24] Still undaunted, Kazan shopped the script around town and was turned down everywhere until, according to Schulberg, the *Hollywood*

Reporter's gossip column informed its readers that a communistic script dealing with waterfront radicals was going nowhere in this town.[25]

In a later letter to Kazan and Schulberg, responding to a Schulberg article in the *New York Times*, Zanuck heatedly denied that he turned down the film because it was a 'touchy' subject: 'I just cannot accept the idea that I lost my courage or gave you a quick brush-off'. While agreeing that 'the advent or debut of CinemaScope was responsible more than anything for my final decision against the property', he reminds them that Brando's participation, which had not yet happened, was a necessity.[26]

As Kazan and Schulberg continued to rewrite the script at the hotel even though Fox was no longer paying for their rooms, fate entered in the flamboyant person of Sam Spiegel, whose room was across the hall. Spiegel, who at this point called himself S. P. Eagle, was a high-living, wheeling and dealing independent producer with a nose for a good property and a penchant for hiring blacklisted or greylisted writers and crews less as a result of his political beliefs than because he could get them more cheaply. Spiegel had formed Horizon Pictures with John Huston in 1947, but the troubled filming of *The African Queen* (1951) had worn down the relationship and Spiegel's most recent film *Melba*, a biography of the Australian opera star directed by Lewis Milestone and starring Patrice Munsel, had lost most of the money he had made on *The African Queen*.[27] More to the point, Spiegel had just arranged funding from United Artists for two unnamed films.[28]

Although Schulberg was flying back to Pennsylvania the next morning, Spiegel asked him to come beforehand at seven o'clock and tell him the plot. With Spiegel virtually invisible under the sheets in his bed, Schulberg paced around, recounting the journey of Terry Malloy, hardly sure that the supine producer was even listening. Finally, Spiegel dropped the bedsheet below his mouth and said 'I'll do it.' By the time they were back in New York Spiegel had set up a budget with United Artists. A thirty-five-day shooting schedule was set and the film was on its way.

Casting presented one big problem: the lead. Brando had been the first choice for the part of Terry Malloy and Zanuck had said early on that without Brando he would not make the film. But Brando's upset over Kazan's HUAC testimony impelled him twice to send the script back unread. John Garfield, Montgomery Clift and Paul Newman had also been possibilities.[29] But Schulberg and Kazan then turned to Frank Sinatra, who had been born in Hoboken and had just won an Academy Award for *From Here to Eternity* that same year. Sam Spiegel later said that he had originally wanted Sinatra to play Father Barry, but Sinatra held out for Terry. With Brando seemingly not interested, Sinatra was told he had the part and was already into wardrobe fittings when Spiegel revealed that he had persuaded Brando to reconsider. Brando said he would do the picture with two provisos, that he be paid $150,000 straight, with no percentage, and that he be allowed to leave the set at 4.00 pm every day for his psychiatrist appointment.[30]

Meanwhile, an experienced technical crew had also been gathered, which included editor Gene Milford, who had won an Academy Award for *Lost Horizon* in 1937, but since then had done mainly B-pictures, and set decorator Richard Day, first hired by Erich von Stroheim, who had won five Oscars, for films such as *How Green Was My Valley* (1941) and *A Streetcar Named Desire*. In accord with his original conception of *Waterfront* as an East Coast movie, Kazan drew heavily for the cast on those performers he had worked with at the Actors Studio. Lee J. Cobb, who had been Willy Loman in *Death of a Salesman*, would be the union boss Johnny Friendly; Karl Malden, the Mitch of *A Streetcar Named Desire*, would be Father Barry; Rod Steiger, who had scored a triumph in the original television version of *Marty*, played Terry's brother Charley the Gent. Many of the others had never been in films or had played only minor parts, while Eva Marie Saint, who was cast as Edie Doyle, had appeared only in a few plays and television programmes.[31]

To complete the atmosphere of authenticity, Schulberg enlisted the help of several of his friends from the boxing world – including Tami Mauriello (Tillio), Tony Galento ('Truck') and Abe Simon (Barney) – to play members of the gang. Hired later as well was Roger Donoghue, an ex-boxer, whose job would be to train Brando, and whose own way of carrying himself helped shape the look of Terry, even perhaps to Brando's pale white make-up and the swollen tender skin above his eyes. As Schulberg recalls, 'Roger had that fair Irish skin that tears easily, with scar tissue around his eyes.'

With Brando finally signed, Spiegel drew up a new budget that United Artists refused to accept, and the picture went to Columbia, although Harry Cohn, who had been barely lukewarm about *The Hook*, was hardly any more enthusiastic about this new waterfront project. Schulberg, Kazan and Spiegel began to work on the script, with Spiegel, according to his biographer, arguing to eliminate the outsider reporter character and pushing for a more internal story and more 'movement' in the plot. Although Schulberg readily admits that he admired Spiegel's sense of plot construction, tempers got so hot that at one point he got up in the middle of the night and began dressing. When his wife asked him what he was doing, he said 'I'm going to kill Sam Spiegel.' The issue was the crucifixion speech Father Barry gives after the murder of 'Kayo' Dugan. It was a speech close to Schulberg's heart because it was taken in great part from the actual speech Father Corridan made to the Knights of Columbus before the 1948 strike. But Spiegel thought it was too long and impeded the action. Finally, after listening to them argue for almost a week, Kazan reassured Spiegel that he would cut it in such a way with interspersed shots and angles that it would play much more quickly. Finally, with a shooting script completed, which would be trimmed further in production, and an $880,000 budget, shooting on the film began on 17 November in the freezing winter of 1953 and wrapped on 26 January 1954 with a few pickup scenes shot later in February.[32]

A Pilgrimage across the River

Although the details are fascinating, delving into the problems of making a film – the tentative steps towards production, the behind-the-camera activity on the set and the decisions about marketing – unavoidably sidelines what is creative and imaginative in a film in favour of the minutiae of its manufacturing process. What may be lost is the film's wholeness, whatever makes it memorable and worth looking at closely to begin with. The helter skelter process of how *On the Waterfront* was put together, the changing circumstances of its independent production, its setting and personnel outside the studio sets and control of Hollywood, along with the real-life pressures of personal political decisions and the daily turmoil on the real waterfront – all this variety and conflict richly orients us towards the film itself.

Schulberg's research had been done on the docks of lower Manhattan. But financial considerations, as well as lack of street noise and other practical factors, shifted the location to Hoboken, on the New Jersey side of the Hudson. A friend of Father Corridan, Austin Tobin, the head of the New York Port Authority, arranged for the use of a pier. In Hoboken, there would also be less interference from the mob, although the production still had to hire the police chief's brother as a bodyguard.

The shift allowed a certain distance from New York in other ways as well, where at the time, as Norman Mailer once noted, there was a general hostility to Kazan, Schulberg and the film among New York left intellectuals.[33] Yet despite Kazan's own alienation from this community, he enlisted artists who would seem to have had similar sympathies, including Boris Kaufman, the youngest brother of the great Soviet filmmaker Dziga Vertov, who had previously only made documentaries in the United States, and Leonard Bernstein, recruited by Spiegel, who wanted another box-office name. Bernstein had at first turned the project down, but then saw a rough cut in February 1954 and signed on. Bernstein was also closely connected to the Adler acting family (Jacob and children Stella and Luther) who had not only been part of the Group Theatre with Kazan but who had also become a surrogate family for Brando when he began studying acting with Stella. Columbia was nervous about Bernstein's own leftist connections, but Kazan, despite his worry that the music made the story too operatic, stuck with him.[34]

A rectilinear slab of a city barely two square miles in size (and a third of that water), referred to by its newspapers as the 'Mile-Square City', Hoboken also allowed a visual detachment from the gaudy grandeur of New York which was appropriate to the plot. Schulberg walked with Kazan along the waterfront scouting locations, 'once we found the little yacht club' that became the gang's hangout, 'we knew this was really the place'. But instead of using the skyscrapers across the river as a glamorous backdrop to the events on the waterfront, Kazan instructed Kaufman 'not to make the skyline of New York picturesque', for in the film there would be the fancy hotels and office buildings from which the marauding hawks swooped down on the pigeons of Hoboken.

In the heights above the river, Hoboken had its own upscale neighbourhoods, where the German immigrants who had helped build the town first settled, to be followed later by a middle-class Italian community. Some of their fancier homes are visible in the background of a few shots in the film. But *On the Waterfront*'s Hoboken is the more

The Hoboken Yacht Club, Johnny Friendly's union office

down-and-out strip on the flats next to the Hudson, where its middle-class inhabitants rarely ventured. The neighbourhood in which the events of the film take place therefore becomes a central part of the film's power, the authentic feel of a real place. Many critics of the film minimise or ignore the setting and discuss *On the Waterfront* primarily in terms of its themes and characters. But when I first saw the film as a teenager, I was struck by the palpable sense of neighbourhood Kazan had embodied in it. Every time I saw the film again, I wondered about this world across the river from New York, from which the Empire State Building and the other skyscrapers of Manhattan appeared like looming and vaguely threatening giants.

In his own film-making, Kazan had discovered this need for an authentic space in which to situate his characters with *Panic in the Streets* (1950), a chase film in which Richard Widmark plays an officer with the US Health Services who races against time to find two carriers of the bubonic plague (Jack Palance and Zero Mostel) loose in New Orleans. The film itself is exciting enough to watch, but what Kazan got out of it, as he recounts, was that for the first time he really

28   Brando with his mother and father and Sam Spiegel (dark overcoat). Another cold day on the set

emphasised a *place*. Previously, his films had been almost entirely shot in the studio and he carried over into them wholesale what he had learned in directing for the stage. But the sense of New Orleans in *Panic in the Streets* was something unique that he felt that movies could do, and that he had to learn. New Orleans wasn't John Ford's Monument Valley, but Kazan was explicitly following Ford's lead and uniting it with a Method acting sense of space – the need to know that actions happen *somewhere* – and that in order to do a scene an actor has to know where he was before he came in.

On the stage that was an acting exercise. But in the freezing temperatures and the rain and snow of Hoboken in the winter of 1953, it was reality. Kazan's daughter Judy, then an eighteen-year-old high-school senior who visited the set several times, has said it was 'an aching, all-permeating cold that seeped up into you from the ground'. After every scene, the actors and crew would huddle around oil-drum fires to keep warm. As Brando cracked, 'It was so damn cold you couldn't overact,' and the viewer can almost feel the cold as Eva Marie Saint hunches Edie's shoulders against the wind. Judy Kazan called it 'very much a hardship location', and was struck by the similarity between the rough clothes and down-and-out look of the actors and extras before the camera and the crew behind it, 'as if we were all working together'. It was a feeling shared by others on the film, especially when Sam Spiegel descended periodically in a fancy overcoat with a showgirl in tow – until Kazan barred him from the set. Like the New York skyscrapers, he too might have been the privileged background against which the film defined itself. Unlike the heat, passion and languor of *Viva Zapata!* or the sun-shower tenderness of *Man on a Tightrope*, the weather of *On the Waterfront* drives feelings and gestures inside – an almost explicit correlative of the stoic repression and 'D 'n D' (deaf and dumb) of the longshoreman's code.

This sense of a real neighbourhood had so enveloped me when I first saw *On the Waterfront* that I resolved to visit Hoboken for myself. Until the late 1960s I had never lived in New York. But for years before when I had visited friends there or driven through, I would always try to use the Holland Tunnel under the Hudson, because every once in a while, craning my neck while driving along that wide street that leads up to the tunnel on the Jersey side, I thought I could see the spires of a Hoboken church I knew must be from *On the Waterfront*. Past the fast-food neon of the strip I also could see the faint outline of trees, perhaps a park, perhaps even the park fronting on the Hudson where Edie

Setting up Joey. Terry tells Joey he'll take the lost pigeon to the roof

The thugs wait for Joey near his roof loft

"I think somebody fell off the roof." Truck, Tillio, Charley, Terry in front of Johnny's bar

"A canary." "Maybe he could sing, but he couldn't fly"

Doyle walked on that misty morning when Father Barry prodded Terry Malloy into telling Edie that he had set her brother Joey up for the kill. 'Honest, Edie, I thought they were just going to lean on him a little.'[35]

On one of those summer days, when I was settling into New York and still hadn't sold my car, I decided it was time to find that place. Its image was fixed in my mind. I knew it was real: the park, that half-finished or half-demolished jetty, the Empire State Building looming unconcerned behind them while Terry doggedly makes his confession over the blast of a boat whistle.

There was no special occasion for the trip, although the twentieth anniversary of *On the Waterfront* would be coming up in a few years. I decided I would cross the river by the Lincoln Tunnel and then make my way down. There are no hills near the water for a while and so there could be no park overlooking it. I reached Hoboken, turned left on 14th Street to Washington, went down Washington and then left on 12th to Hudson, which seemed to be the end.

I found a park between 10th and 11th on Hudson that overlooks the river. At the top of the park, next to the American Can/Maxwell House plant whose sign was visible from Manhattan at night, a street curves off down to the river – River Road, perhaps the River Street of the film, I thought, the site of Johnny Friendly's saloon.

I parked half a block away from the park that seemed so right, but unsure of my bearings because there was no church fronting on the park. How could Terry and Edie have run out of the church, escaping from the goons who have broken up Father Barry's meeting, met the homeless guy in the park who refuses to be bought off by Terry, talked by the swings after Edie drops her glove, and finally wound up in front of the fence, while New York sat impassive across the river?

Further south, at 4th and Hudson, is another park, and this one did have a church fronting it, Sts Peter and Paul, blockish, yellow-brick, hardly the imposing edifice of the film. But here there was no way to stand at a fence and flirt obliquely because a Little League field and open showers were in the way. Yet below the park, River Road, run-down and almost empty, had turned into River Street, facing a block filled with decaying piers. A few saloons were open below the gutted and windowless houses. I stepped into the Holland House for a beer and asked the bartender, who was watching a soap opera on television whether *On the Waterfront* was shot here.

'Oh yeah, right here. The pigeon loft was two doors down.'

'How about the bar?' I asked.

'That'll be Vandenberg's, 314. But he's sold out.'

The sign over Vandenberg's says 'Pepe's'. Inside it was bare of all fixtures, but three men sat in front of the bar and Pepe Vandenberg stood behind, dispensing beer from a sixpack as if nothing had changed. After a little annoyance at the stranger invading his afternoon, Pepe allowed that this in fact was the bar from *On the Waterfront*.

I tell ya, I didn't want to do it. I got enough trouble without renting the bar to some movie company. But Kazan came in here and looked around with that thing to his eye, the viewfinder, and said he had to have this place. Then they came back with Marotta the police chief. I'm gonna chase the chief of police out?

Gradually, he warmed to the subject.

Hoboken, late 1960s. Neighbourhood children posing in front of the Doyle apartment building, since torn down

Hoboken, late 1960s. Johnny Friendly's bar, since torn down

The only thing left from the movie is that dent over there on the wall. That's where Brando threw the gun at the picture. That was some scene. I was behind the counter and Kazan said 'Say whatever you want. Say shit on the whole scene. It won't matter. You don't have a mike. But say something.' They did six takes on that scene because Malden kept muffing his lines. You know where he says 'Anybody can take a .38 and put some lead into human flesh'? Well, he kept saying .45 instead of .38. They swore like thieves, those actors. Every time Malden said .45 instead of .38, he'd say, 'For Christ's sake, I fucked it up again,' and him in those priest clothes. It was really something to see.

Finally Kazan walked up to him, and he's small and Karl is pretty big, and Kazan slapped him in the mouth twice and said 'You're not paying any attention, now walk.' And he made him walk up and down between the bar and the phone booth. Finally, he shot the scene again and Malden was really mad and it came out right.

Terry and Barry confront each other in Johnny's bar

After convincing Terry to testify, Barry offers him a beer

Brando was a bum. The only decent actor there was Lee Cobb. The first time I heard him talk, I thought, what's this, we got a fairy in this bar? Then he got on camera. I wouldn't get within ten feet of that guy, he sounded so tough. He was really good.

After that bar scene Brando came over to the other end of the bar where my wife and her sister and my mother-in-law were sitting to apologise. He said we actors use profanity to relax, instead of getting all wound up inside. He did apologise. That I'll say for him.

So not only was this the bar, it turns out, but all the men here, including Pepe, had been extras. Gradually, as they reminisced, I started putting together the reality of the location with the sense of neighbourhood the film had created for me. It turned out that the park scene was actually pieced together from three parks, a daring thing for a director to do on a tight shooting schedule.[36] When Terry asks Edie if she remembers him from grade school, he's standing in one park. When she replies, she is standing in another, some ten blocks away. And when Father Barry later encourages Terry to tell Edie that he was the one who set up Joey, Brando makes an impossible journey to her that in reality goes over a high iron fence and down a hill that ends at the top of a fifteen-foot sheer wall on the park side of River Street.

When I saw the film again, I could see how it was done. What had appeared visually seamless, had actually been put together by Kazan, Kaufman and the editor Gene Milford, using the ability of Brando, Saint and Malden to bridge time and space with their performances. The gaps between actual spaces, the ruptures between scenes shot at different times, had somehow melded into an emotional experience of a neighbourhood and its people so cohesive one could almost draw a map.

Of course, all traditional narrative films try to make the cuts invisible and create the illusion of a continuous space. But here particularly that illusion is connected to the ethos of a community, the illusory comfort of D 'n D and the embrace of the group. An essential part of both the visual texture and the verbal themes is the way Terry finally tries to break out of it – after a fashion.

Hope may seem to reside in the openness of the water and the rooftop pigeon loft. But the dark streets and narrow spaces of the bar, the saloon and the apartments signal a gloomy fatality as well. The scene in which Terry and Edie are chased down a narrow alley by a truck bent on obliterating them takes place in reality on a back street wide enough for two, almost three, such trucks to fit.[37] But the lighting and Kaufman's

Edie and Terry try to outrun the truck bent on killing them

Hoboken, late 1960s.
Court Street and
Charley's Wall without
the benefit of Boris
Kaufman's lighting

As the truck passes, light
falls on Charley's dead
body, hung from a
longshoreman's hook

Close-up of the dead
Charley cut from many
European prints

Terry with the gun Charley
gave him, walking off to
seek revenge

camerawork turns the real place into a noir nightmare, as the truck's headlights reveal the body of Charley, and Terry begins to move inexorably towards his confrontation with Johnny Friendly. Like the early scene in which a policeman tries to cover Joey Doyle's body with newspapers, or the shot of the mobster Tillio guarding the garage door through which Charley Malloy goes to his death, the brightly lit foreground and the dark, almost impenetrable background, is visually reminiscent of the harsh and unsentimental newspaper photographs of murder and mayhem shot by the pioneering photojournalist Weegee and included in his book, *Naked City* (1945), which helped inspire such films as *Naked City* (Jules Dassin, 1948) and *Call Northside 777* (Henry Hathaway, 1948).[38]

In scenes like this, the film creates a visually unforgiving environment, a seemingly closed system of behaviour and moral manners in which D 'n D is the etiquette and stoicism the philosophy. 'No matter how much we hate the torpedos, we wouldn't rat on them to an outsider.' This is the world that Pop Doyle has sent Edie away from, to St Ann's Catholic school up the Hudson in Tarrytown – a more protected world, on the palisades above the river rather than right next to it. But along with the need to break away from it, the neighbourhood has a kind of centripetal force that brings people back in, as it has Edie. At the end of the film, when she pleads with Terry, rejected by all sides, to walk away from it, to 'go someplace we can live in peace', he can't stand the thought of living on a farm ('I don't like the country. The crickets make me nervous') and has to return to the fray.

Kayo Dugan tells Father
Barry the D 'n D
philosophy

Joey's Jacket and Edie's Glove

> I used to get there at dawn all alone and walk around the waterfront of Hoboken. I got ideas from the docks, the river. Even the cold gives you ideas. ... I hope the story that I'm telling has so many overtones that it becomes symbolic of our time, of our issues, which is to say mythic.[39]

For all its realistic atmosphere and neighbourhood specificity, *On the Waterfront* traffics deeply in symbols, most obviously Joey Doyle's jacket, the mantle that is passed along first from Pop Doyle to Kayo Dugan, who will become the next informant or truth-teller to the Waterfront Crime Commission, and finally passed to Terry Malloy by Edie after Dugan's murder in the hold. After his own testimony, Terry puts on the jacket to go down to the shape-up 'and get my rights'.

Christian symbolism lays a heavy hand on American post-war film and fiction. Every crossed window pane is pressed to yield a crucifix, every rainfall a baptism, every sunrise a sign of rebirth and every victim a potential Christ-figure. Explicitly Christian-era epics such as *Quo Vadis?* (1951), *The Robe* (1953) and *Demetrius and the Gladiators* (1954) drew huge audiences; unfriendly-turned-friendly witness Edward Dmytryk directed *Give Us This Day* (1949), based on the novel, *Christ in Concrete*; and blacklisted writer–director Jules Dassin made *He Who Must Die* (1957) about a village Passion play in 1920s' Greece that becomes real.[40] In literature, William Faulkner's *A Fable*, which won the Pulitzer Prize in the same year *On the Waterfront* was released, transposed the Gospel story to the trenches of World War I, while Ernest Hemingway's *The Old Man and the Sea*, rife with images of Christian suffering and endurance, was specifically mentioned in his Nobel Prize citation of the same year. Meanwhile literary critics counselled students how to search for the *deus absconditus* in modernist texts, and essays on the imagery of apocalypse and healing waters filled the learned journals.

Using Christian imagery to interpret *On the Waterfront* raises an even trickier issue, since one of the main characters is a priest, with his occupational commitment to a meaning beyond the immediate, the need to go outside the social context for both an individual and a religious truth. This urge to make the Gospel message immediately relevant was one of the things that had attracted Schulberg to Father Corridan, the ability to find transcendence in the details of everyday life: 'Christ is in the shape-up ... He's walking beside you.' But as the script developed, many of the explicitly Christian trappings were eliminated. In an early version dated April 1951 called *Crime on the Waterfront*, for example, the group kneeling around a body crushed by a falling barrel is described as being like 'an impressionistic religious painting, giving it a fuzzy, holy quality'.

Similarly, the wandering homeless beggar Mutt, who in earlier scripts is a kind of chorus muttering analogies with the Passion whenever a death occurs, becomes a more realistically presented character in the film. In effect, instead of being a pervasive and unquestioned view of the world, Christianity in *On the Waterfront* is a perspective specifically rooted in the character of Father Barry and, less centrally, in his parishioners.

What kind of symbol then is Joey's jacket? It's not quite like Father Barry's view of symbols, in which everything that happens can be referred to a system of Christian imagery. 'It's a crucifixion,' Barry says in his powerful sermon after Dugan's death, blending the trouble on the docks with the death of Christ. After Joey's murder at the beginning of the film, he had tried to comfort Edie by telling her she can 'find me in the church'. 'In the church? In the church?' she screams. 'Since when did a saint hide in a church?' Stung by her reproach, Barry has brought his spiritual values out into a harsher world, and, as the hoist brings him out of the hold, Pop Doyle hands him a crumpled cigarette, the sacrament the world gives him, instead of the other way around.

Terry, by contrast, is a creature solely of the immediate. 'Hey, Killer, you have to get some ambition,' says his brother Charley. 'All I need is a couple of potatoes,' responds Terry dismissively. From one point of view, Terry's journey in the film is from that no-tomorrow view

'Since when did a saint hide in a church'

The shape-up. Pop Doyle passes Joey's jacket to K. O. Dugan

Dugan zips up the jacket just before the load of whiskey is dropped on him

Luke gives Joey's jacket back to Edie after Dugan's death

Back from the hearings where he has testified, Terry takes Joey's jacket and tells Edie, "I'm just gonna go down there and get my rights"

Wearing Joey's jacket, Terry calls out Johnny Friendly for their final confrontation

Barry zips up Terry's jacket after the beating: "Finish what you started"

of life to appreciating some larger, more general morality, as instilled in him by Father Barry and Edie, and Christian symbolism easily fits into the framework of such a conversion narrative. With this interpretation in mind, numerous critics have mocked Terry's final stumbling walk down the dock to face the ship owner in his fancy overcoat as a pseudo-Calvary, another effort to ennoble the informer by laying on Christian imagery. But in addition to Kazan's own frequent denial of any specific religious belief, it should be remembered that it is Father Barry, the professional symboliser who encourages and even manipulates Terry into making the walk ('Johnny Friendly is layin' odds that you won't get up') and insists that no one help him along the way.[41]

A more fruitful way of looking at symbols in Kazan's films of this period is to distinguish between symbols that refer to an external belief system and symbols created by the characters themselves as a way of giving their lives meaning and purpose. Unlike Jesus's cloak in *The Robe*, and that film's story of what happened to one of the soldiers who played dice on it, Joey's jacket is a much more home-made symbol. 'Kayo' Dugan accepts it from Joey's father because it is better than his own. 'Mine has more holes than the Pittsburgh infield.' The jacket also fits into a larger pattern in the film of clothes and coverings that is totally apparent to all the characters and reflects a waterfront reality. 'You think I'm just a gravy train rider in a turned-around collar,' Father Barry says to Edie when she doubts his commitment to finding Joey's murderers. Tommy, the kid who follows Terry around and finally turns against him after he testifies, wears a 'Golden Warriors' jacket. In contrast to Joey's workaday jacket and Tommy's with its embroidered Golden Warriors' logo, the

The shipping executive at the end of the film, another powerful man in a fancy overcoat

The shape-up. Terry and the representative of the Waterfront Crime Commission (Leif Erickson): "I don't know nuttin. I aint seen nuttin, and I aint sayin nuttin"

A characteristic Kazan triangular setup: Pop Doyle, Dugan, and the loan shark J.P.

Father Barry and Edie. "I suppose you think I'm just a gravy train rider with a turned around collar"

Edie and Terry meet as she tries to get a work tab for her father. "Things are lookin up on the docks"

gangsters running the union all wear fancy overcoats. To Barry, they are 'killers in camel hair coats' and the film's ending gathers much of its ambiguity from the image of Terry leading the men into a dock fronted by a ship owner wearing a coat indistinguishable from Johnny Friendly's (or Sam Spiegel's).

On the edge in so many ways, Terry is also caught visually between the fancy overcoats of the gang and the equally well-dressed investigators from the Crime Commission. He is comfortable with neither world, and after his testimony, he returns home in a suit with an obviously ripped jacket. To both Johnny Friendly's gang and the D 'n D longshoremen, he is a turncoat.

Clothes are a kind of armour, not just against the cold that suffuses the film, but also against other sorts of vulnerability. Big Mac, the pier boss, zips up his jacket just before giving the signal to drop the crates of Scotch on 'Kayo' Dugan, and Father Barry zips up Terry's jacket as he persuades him to make the walk that ends the film. Although almost everyone in the film talks about 'guts', the visual message, like the stiff upper lip of D 'n D, is to maintain a manly surface, keep the leaking wounds invisibly inside.

Such visual symbols also play the role of anchoring otherwise more general themes. As Kazan comments marginally on one version of the script, 'Is it being over-told? Can it be boiled down to just pix?' An essential part of his own directing method in theatre was the emphasis on objects. In *Streetcar*, for example, he created a subtext of physical objects to parallel the text.[42] With this technique, he was closer to Stella Adler's view of Stanislavsky, in which actions precede emotions, than to Lee Strasberg's, in which emotions precede actions. Strasberg's stress on affective memory, the term for using an actor's past personal emotion to invest a character, always ran the danger of making the performer's own psychic history the cohesion of a scene rather than the character's development within the play or script. By contrast, action and especially objects – knowing the space in which the character lived and the things that define him there – brought the performer back to the immediacy of the work. As Brando remarks in one of the few comments about craft in his autobiography, 'An actor's motivation often depends on focusing sharply on details.'[43]

Frequently hostile to what he considered to be Strasberg's view of acting, Brando had studied with Adler before he came to the Studio and his own work furnishes some interesting examples of this use of details and setting. In both *Zapata* and *On the Waterfront*, for example, he has a troubled relation with an older brother. In both plots the brother is killed and in both, Brando's character has to convey anguish over the death at the same time as mixed emotions over his relation to him. While he bends over Anthony Quinn's body in *Zapata*, the pain in his face is anchored physically by the way he picks dirt or lint or some smudge from his brother's clothes, an act of almost motherly tenderness that complicates the manly need to be the stoic leader. In *On the Waterfront*, before vowing revenge, he lovingly drapes Charley's arms over his shoulders to take the dead body off the wall, then checks the gun to make sure cartridges are in all the chambers.

A more celebrated moment in which objects convey emotional nuance occurs in *On the Waterfront* after the meeting in the church basement is broken up by Johnny Friendly's goons and Terry shows Edie an escape route. This sequence involves another piece of clothing, this time Edie's glove. The scene has been recounted often, and, watching the film, the sequence unfolds so inevitably that it hard to realise that its centrepiece was a rehearsal accident. In the shooting script the encounter occurs at night, but in the film it is misty day, perhaps early morning, and Boris Kaufman has given this and other scenes some of the grainy quality that marked his work with Vigo in *L'Atalante*. In the park, the neighbourhood drunk Mutt has just virtually accused Terry of complicity in the death of Joey ('You wuz there that night') and Terry pushes him away. But Mutt has the last word: 'You're still a bum.'[44]

'What did that man mean?' asks Edie, her eyes nervously darting from one side to the other. But Terry begins to steer their conversation away from these dangerous waters. 'Are you training to be a nun?' he asks. As they walk across the park, he asks her about the school in Tarrytown, up the Hudson river, where she's a student. Edie nervously begins to take her little white woollen gloves out of her coat pocket, and in the process drops one. Terry picks it up and begins absentmindedly to hold it while he speaks and she makes abrupt little gestures to try to get it back. Pulling out the glove's fingers and picking lint from it, Terry settles himself on the swing, talks about how he admires brains, and puts the glove on his own hand. They walk farther, he talks about remembering her as a young girl in school with braces and braids, and then he stops and offers to walk her home. 'I can get home myself,' she says, pulling the glove off his hand. 'You don't remember me, do you?' he asks, and she responds, 'I remembered you the first moment I saw you.'

Karl Malden has said he was on the set that day and this all happened on camera. But Eva Marie Saint says that it had happened accidentally in rehearsal and then was retained for the shooting.

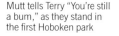

Mutt tells Terry "You're still a bum," as they stand in the first Hoboken park

I don't believe in improvisation while the camera is running. That's not really art. Marlon picked up the glove in rehearsal. Another actor would have just given it back. But Marlon would never do any scene quite the same. It was exciting, like being in a play. It became the catalyst to keep me in the scene. Why should Edie, with her strict upbringing stay with a member of the opposite sex? That was the problem of the scene.

Whatever the actual genesis of the interplay, it works perfectly on screen. Dropping the glove seems like a total accident, but instead of responding conventionally, Terry begins to play unconsciously with it. 'He put it on his hand in a very sensual way,' Saint remarks. Edie nervously responds to what he does and the dialogue moves on, now anchored in a physical object that conveys its own nuanced meanings. As Kazan says in his autobiography, 'I didn't direct that; it happened, just as it might have in an improvisation at the Actors Studio.'[45]

Kazan once remarked that the technique it takes a lifetime to learn as a director is when to direct and when not to direct.

The first thing for a director is to see what a talent does on its own. It may be, as it frequently was with Marlon, better than anything you can describe. ... If you don't get what you want, then start directing – but not until then.[46]

Casting therefore was a crucial element in Kazan's preparation for a film, a procedure totally unlike, say, Hitchcock's, in which the director's total vision of the film dictated a more condescending attitude towards the actors as objects themselves. If improvisation could happen, then the director is not so much an aesthetic authority as he is an ally with the performer in making the scene, and the film, work. As Kazan has said about helping an inexperienced actor, in particular, 'You stay on his side of the camera, sometimes physically during rehearsal, but spiritually at all times.'[47] By the same token, the work of such a director will have its own somewhat jaundiced view of authority in general, aligning itself with the subversive individual rather than the big picture.

Creating an environment in which accidents will happen that are in accord with the themes and movements of the story corresponds as well to what Kazan, following Stanislavsky, has called objectives. Because film is a more temporally disjointed medium than theatre, in which scenes are rarely shot in the sequence in which they will finally appear, there is more

"What did that man mean just now?" asks Edie in another misty park

Terry picks up Edie's dropped glove and absentmindedly picks off lint

Still talking, Terry sits down on a swing and starts to pull on the glove

Edie nervously reaches for the glove, while Terry talks about Charley: "Personally I admire brains"

Edie finally manages to take the glove from a puzzled Terry

"I remembered you the first moment I saw you." Edie in the park overlooking River St., Manhattan dimly visible in the background

need for an actor to embody the character, knowing and even sometimes conveying in a particular scene where it has come from and where it is going. In the glove scene, as Terry and Edie get to know each other, they move from the present into the past, back to their innocent youth, an innocence being severely tested for Edie and starting to be recaptured for Terry. The park itself is a more open, more natural space, and its childhood swings help set the scene and complement the dialogue. Brando's open-mouthed gum chewing adds another visual nuance, an artificial effort at nonchalance, a glimpse into the childlike side of Terry. Between the two of them, the memory of younger days and less cynical responses can begin to emerge, in particular for Terry.

The glove adds the crucial element of interchange. Edie and Terry are not just trading reminiscences. They are beginning to trade attitudes. He puts on her glove as he tries out, and will continue to explore, her view of the world. When she takes it back, it will have the memory of his hand in it. These are such fragile symbolic nuances that to mention them in cold print threatens to overwhelm their delicacy. But they are definitely there, just as there is also something unavoidably sexual implied when Terry puts his boxer's hand into this glove that inadvertently popped out of Edie's otherwise nunnish outfit.

Connected to self-made symbols like Joey's jacket or Edie's glove are the subjective moments in the film, for example, when the waterfront pile-driver pounds violently and a steam whistle blasts while Terry makes a confession that Edie doesn't want to hear. In the immediate context this background noise overwhelming the foreground dialogue solves a plot problem: Kazan and Schulberg were walking down by the river wondering what to do with this dramatic moment of confession in which Terry tells Edie something that the audience knows already. They heard a steam whistle from a passing ocean liner and said, 'That's it.' It's realistic, something that could happen in Hoboken, part of the sounds of the neighbourhood.

But the moment also stresses Edie's horror at the confession: her desire not to hear is as great as Terry's need to speak. She puts her gloved hands over her ears, and then her mouth. Although he speaks in close-up, neither she nor the audience can really hear him. Such moments where poetry and realism come together give a mythic aura to the otherwise semi-documentary tone of the gangster plot. After what Kazan referred to as the 'perfection' of *Panic in the Streets* ('It's easy. It didn't try to do much') or the moral clarities of *Gentleman's Agreement*, *On the Waterfront* daringly mixes its styles and its themes. In earlier scripts, for

Terry confesses his role in Joey's murder to Father Barry

Barry watches as Terry confesses to Edie amid the waterfront rubble

Edie's reaction to Terry's confession

The rumpled cigarette pulled from Barry's pocket conveys his own upset

example, Schulberg notes several dissolves, but they have disappeared from the film. While visually exploring the romantic and mythic aspects of the plot, Kazan cuts from scene to scene in a more documentary style befitting his cinematographer Boris Kaufman. Time and the plot move briskly and inexorably onward.

With this mingled commitment to the realistic and the mythic, Kazan might be seen as standing between or combining the social preoccupations of Arthur Miller with the individual psychology of Tennessee Williams. Williams's *The Glass Menagerie* (1945) virtually announced itself as a polemic against the theatrical realism that had been the standard of Broadway theatre in the 1930s. It emphasised the subjectivity of the characters on stage and had scenes that were occurring in the mind of a character more than in some fourth-wall setting. But at the same time it resembled stylised plays from the 1930s like *Waiting for Lefty* which walked a line between realistic content and a heightened presentation. At first, when Williams praised Kazan's directions of *All My Sons* and sent *A Streetcar Named Desire* to him, Kazan was dubious and Williams himself said that he knew Kazan was always looking for a 'thesis'. But *Streetcar* moved Kazan away from visual and thematic certainties and gave his work a new psychological dimension that meshed perfectly the next year with Miller's more psychological *Death of a Salesman*, itself, as Miller has said, heavily influenced by the poetic realism of *Streetcar*.

On stage, the slippery passage between immediate reality, memory and fantasy could be mediated by Jo Mielziner's sets, in which solid walls suddenly became transparent and permeable. But how would this work in film with its seemingly irreducible physical reality? Just as in theatre Kazan's dramatic imagination is divided between Miller's common-man realism and Williams's common-man fantasy, the way he creates visual meaning in his films always occupies some ground between the specific and the transcendent, the observed detail and the poetic meaning. Superficially, *On the Waterfront* has a generic kinship with the Oscar-winning Best Film of the next year, *Marty*. Shot on location in black and white, it too deals with normal, unglamorous people. But *Marty* never strays from its origins as a television play about a lower-middle-class world, while Kazan's brand of realism often seems to invite moments that are more self-reflexive and self-conscious, not only about the events of the story but also about the film-making process itself. Why, say, does he permit actor James Westerfield (Big Mac) to call his own name during the shape-up as one of the dockworkers favoured for the day? And why is

Terry with Edie at the Garden bar. "You want to hear my philosophy of life? Do it to him before he does it to you"

Filled with guilt, Terry says, "Edie, I'd like to help"

Unaware that Terry has any role in her brother's death, Edie strokes Terry's face: "You would if you could"

one of the union officers named at the Crime Commission hearing Mladen Sekulovich, Karl Malden's real name? In-jokes perhaps, but references outward that hardly stand alone in the film. In the midst of real locations and brutal events, they remind the viewer that this is a movie.

A more extended reach outside the film occurs in the crucial scene at the Garden bar, where Terry and Edie sit down for the drink she has never had before, and they begin to share tentatively their views of the world, foreshadowed in the glove scene. Terry at first cannot believe that Edie cares to hear the story of his orphan life and career as a fighter. 'Shouldn't everybody care about everybody else?' she asks. 'What a fruitcake you are!' he says in amazement, and after she repeats the sentiment, he gets tough. 'Want to hear my philosophy of life?' says Terry. 'Do it to him before he does it to you.' 'I never met anyone like you,' responds Edie. 'There's not a spark of sentiment or romance, or human kindness in your whole body.' 'What good does it do for you, except get you in trouble?' They continue to spar, but along the way Terry inadvertently reveals his guilty conscience about the murder of Joey. 'That Father Barry, I didn't like the way he was lookin' at me.' 'He was looking at everybody the same way,' replies Edie.

As far as words are concerned, this part of the scene ends in a stalemate, and Edie gets up to leave. But she is frightened by the raucous wedding party in the bar's main room and Terry offers to walk her home. Bernstein's love theme, which we previously have heard only on the soundtrack is now being played by a muted trumpet in the wedding party orchestra. 'It's a pretty tune,' Edie says, and Terry asks her to dance. What can't be accomplished in language might work in the play of music and bodies. For a moment they are in harmony, about to kiss among the leafy plants that edge the dance floor, recapturing some of the natural innocence they first touched in the park.

But the brutal present intervenes. First, a goon from Johnny Friendly's gang tells Terry that Johnny wants to see him. Showing off before Edie that he's his own man, Terry says he'll come when he's ready, after walking Edie home. Then one of the Crime Commission investigators comes over and serves Terry a subpoena, which he rips up. 'I won't eat cheese for no cops, that's for sure.' Suddenly Edie realises that Terry is implicated in Joey's death and, after calling Terry a bum, she runs out of the room.

This complex sequence illustrates one of Kazan's basic tenets of film-making: 'Look for the contradictions' – the contradictions within a character, the contradictions of tone within a scene, and between scenes.

Before shooting started, Brando had asked him to clarify the difference between Terry Malloy and Stanley Kowalski as characters and Kazan wrote a long letter explaining his view: Stanley is surrounded by friends, the centre of attention; Terry is alone, an orphan, who fights for recognition. 'Boxing is Terry's armor and his defense. ... It is a complex part. Not a strong color without the next moment the opposite coming up. ... a combination of primitivism and gentleness, of false swagger and painful self doubt.'

From his bravado and her naiveté at the beginning of the Garden sequence, both Terry and Edie go through a whole kaleidoscope of emotional changes until in the last shot we see him bereft and alone. But immediately after the glare and noise of the bar scene, we are on a dark street, where Terry in long-shot walks, idly tossing a stone and whistling the same love theme that had moved from the soundtrack to the bar orchestra and helped set the stage for the dance between Terry and Edie. Abruptly he will be accosted by a car full of Johnny Friendly, brother Charley and assorted thugs, which makes a u-turn next to him with a screech and thump of tyres. But for the moment Terry had been somewhere with Edie, and his expanding awareness, his unconscious feeling that there may be a bigger picture is signalled almost subliminally to us (and perhaps to him) by Bernstein's score.[48]

The surprising thing is that such 'cinematic' moments do not undermine the general realistic look and feel of the film. Like the refusal of fourth-wall theatrical realism in both *Streetcar* and *Salesman*, they enhance it. Paradoxically, while most self-conscious gestures in film distance us ironically from what's happening, a sequence like this brings us closer to the characters and their feelings. The tension between the social problem film with its semi-documentary detail and the poetic exploration of character remains an unresolved and therefore energising element in *On the Waterfront*. Luckily, one documentary element was considered and then dropped: a helicopter shot of the entire New York harbour descending to the gangster clubhouse that would begin the film. The cameraman James Wong Howe scouted locations for such a shot in March 1954. I have been unable to discover whose idea it was and whether it was ever actually filmed. But opening the film with such an omniscient overview would have destroyed its carefully built empathy with the characters. After Kazan had cast many actual longshoremen as extras and recruited an ensemble of actors who could themselves have emerged from the tenements of Hoboken, it would seem strange to begin the film with a shot that was so explicitly condescending.[49]

Kazan's own desire for authenticity, together with his admiration of the neo-realist use of non-professionals and a careful attention to the reality of their lives, keeps the camera in an intimate relation with the performers. Psychological reality was complemented by casting people who actually looked like the characters they played. This was the style and the attitude embodied in the name 'Group Theatre' and which in the beginning animated the Actors Studio, until Lee Strasberg's pre-occupation with stars like Marilyn Monroe undermined its idealism. Not that the Group was immune to the problem of the star turn versus the collaborative effort. No matter how much repertory was stressed and roles rotated, no matter how much Hollywood-successful actors like Franchot Tone were made to feel guilty about deserting the cause, there was always a pressure towards mainstream success and Broadway production that necessarily helped create stars.

The collective politics of the 1930s to a certain extent kept these tensions in balance. In the post-war period, with American society generally looking for new faces and new styles of being, the urge towards the star became more overwhelming. More obviously than theatre, movies were a star system, and however much someone like Brando began and remained hostile to award ceremonies and self-promotion, he was whistling in the wind. Starting as an actor but turning into a star, he himself in the latter part of his career would do virtuoso turns, even in secondary roles, as if there were no one else on the screen or in the plot but himself. As a star he could no longer do what he had done so well preparing for *On the Waterfront* – hang out with the longshoremen, the people he was trying to portray, melt into the crowd and just watch.

But another remarkable achievement of *On the Waterfront* is how much it succeeds in re-creating something like the collaborative efforts of the past. For all the talk of the Method and the theory of acting that sur-rounds the film, this is acting that does not stand out or telegraph to the audience 'I'm doing a great job of playing this character who is unlike me and whose accent and look is not really my own.' Not only are the major players steeped in their milieu, but the minor characters as well have a kind of weighty authenticity. The professional boxers recruited by Schulberg to play gangsters bring their own physical presence to their roles, while when one comes across actors such as John Hamilton (Pop Doyle) and James Westerfield (Big Mac) in other films, they have little of the same per-suasiveness. Even relatively minor characters like the Crime Commission investigators (Leif Erickson and Martin Balsam) still get a focus of camera attention that grounds the main story in social and psychological detail, while many with even less screen time, even no lines at all (like Nehemiah Persoff as the taxi driver who takes brother Charley to his death after the 'contender' scene) make a lasting impression. As Kazan frequently remarked, casting for him was ninety per cent of the equation. Once the look of the character was set and Kazan felt he had an empathy with the actor's inner life, the rest could fall into place. To the end of his life his two main criticisms of Hollywood were that no one was making the kind of political movies he did and in a star-obsessed system the need to match character with face and body was being ignored. As his son Nick recalls, when he was shown *Schindler's List*, he stopped watching after twenty minutes and said with some irritation: 'No one looked that way then.'

Like the grimy, work-aged appearance of many of the longshoremen, the prosperous look of both Lee J. Cobb and Rod Steiger ground their performances – the fancy clothes, the pinky rings and other signs of glitzy respectability, the cheeks so smooth-shaven you could almost see the razor burn. But to the look is added action. In another of Kazan's maxims, directing turns psychology into behaviour.

> You don't ever talk about the emotion [with actors]. All that does is tense an actor up. What you talk about is what they want out of a scene – why they are going into it. ... If you talk about what their character is feeling, you get nothing but simulated emotions.[50]

Movement, gesture, voice and facial expressions express changes of mind in ways that might even be unclear to the characters themselves. Arthur Miller remarked about Kazan as a director at the time of *After the Fall* that he had an 'organic sense of the connection between any individual moment and the thematic statement of a play. ... he always tries to make a whole of opposites.'[51] The point of a character then is not to be 'read' in any simple way, and it is interesting to note that much of what Kazan cuts from Schulberg's script (and much of what Schulberg puts back into his novel *Waterfront*) makes otherwise submerged aspects of character explicit, like Terry's attitude towards women.

In this less explicit depiction of character, Steiger's Charley especially has a histrionic tone that masks his own precarious position in the gang, while Cobb invests Johnny Friendly with an affable brutality that easily erupts into violence. Steiger is of course most on display in the taxi scene. The self-confidence in his plump, clean-shaven face and the jaunty scarf at his throat gradually disintegrating as he realises how he has betrayed Terry in the name of helping him, and that this may lead

Charley and Terry in the taxicab: "Maybe you shouldn't be on the outside so much"

"A steady job and a couple extra potatoes, that's all I want"

"Listen to me, Terry, Take the job. No questions. Just take it"

Terry pushes the gun aside: "Charley, oh Charley ... Wow." Brando balked at this scene as unrealistic until Kazan suggested the solution of pushing the gun aside

Terry remembers when Charley told him to throw the fight against Wilson: "This aint your night"

"I coulda been a contender. I coulda been somebody ..."

inevitably to Terry's death and his own. Similarly, Johnny Friendly's abrupt attack in the early bar scene on Skins, who has been holding out payoff money, not only shows the different sides of Johnny's character but also, because it arrives late in the scriptwriting process, may indicate how much Kazan seeks to build shifting a complex emotional tone into a scene. From his self-glorification as a soft touch to the beating of Skins to tenderly tucking a fifty-dollar bill in Brando's shirt collar, Cobb smoothly shifts from one colour to another.

'A pigeon for a pigeon'

> I finally decided to do the film, but what I didn't realize then was that *On the Waterfront* was really a metaphorical argument by Gadg and Budd Schulberg; they made the film to justify finking on their friends.[52]

The received interpretation of *On the Waterfront* has so stressed the issue of informing and so concertedly tried to parallel the testimony of Kazan and Schulberg with that of Terry Malloy that it has virtually obliterated what was actually going on in the New York and New Jersey docks before and even during the time the film was being made. The traditional view is perhaps most succinctly summed up by Victor Navasky in *Naming Names*:

> [*On the Waterfront*] makes the definitive case for the HUAC informer or at least is – among its considerable other achievements – a valiant attempt to complicate the public perception of the issue. ... Whatever else it may be, *Waterfront* seems an allegory for 1950s anti-Communism, with the Waterfront Crime Commission an analog for HUAC ...[53]

But to focus on their testimony as the 'real' meaning of the film ignores the very immediate issues the film deals with. The parallel many critics drew between the Friendly mob and Communists is particularly ironic since 'Communist' was exactly what ILA president Joseph P. Ryan would shout every time his corrupt rule of the longshoreman's union was threatened. If for the conspiracy view of *On the Waterfront*, Terry is the Kazan/Schulberg surrogate ratting on his Communist brethren, in the cutting edge of more immediate current events, he is either the 'Communist' insurgent revolting against the cosy relation of union

"A pigeon for a pigeon." Terry finds all of his racing pigeons dead

A weeping Tommy has killed them in revenge for his testimony

leaders and ship owners, or perhaps the disciple of the fire-breathing anti-ILA priest Father Corridan.[54]

From 1945 to 1954, the New York waterfront was constantly in the news. William O'Dwyer, the district attorney who declined to pursue the Pete Panto murder case despite grand jury testimony about the involvement of the Brooklyn waterfront mob, was mayor from 1945 to 1950 and actively supported the union regime of ILA president Joseph Ryan. At the same time, William 'Big Bill' McCormack, the head of one of the big shipping lines, was freely referred to in newspaper columns and magazine articles as the 'Mr Big' of the waterfront for his role in brokering the deals between the unions and the owners.[55]

On the Waterfront is therefore that rarity among American films, and especially among Academy Award-winners, a film that deals directly with a specific contemporary social problem and one that affects the working class rather than the middle class. As the script was being written and revised, events on the waterfront were moving forward as well: insurgent longshoremen were being beaten up and murdered, vast quantities of merchandise were being stolen ('You know how the boss feels about individual pilferage'), and ex-convicts who had been convicted of a wide variety of violent crimes were given ILA union cards and appointed to positions of power in the locals. In 1951 the Congressional Crime Commission headed by Senator Estes Kefauver called the ILA 'infested with hoodlums', and in the same year Daniel Bell wrote an article for *Fortune* magazine that later became a chapter in his book *The End of Ideology* called 'The Racket-Ridden Longshoremen'.

Whatever the analogies then, between Kazan and Schulberg testifying and Terry Malloy doing the same, the characterisation of mob power over the unions in *On the Waterfront* is no mere scrim for some other set of issues. Communism did exist on the waterfront, but among the rebels rather than the union officials. In fact, according to labour historians of the period, its influence had waned by the time of the 1948 strike, when Father Corridan was called on the carpet by the Archbishop of New York, Francis Cardinal Spellman, to respond to accusations that he had started the strike. As Colin J. Davis comments, 'Although bitterly opposed to one another, the two organizations [the Communist Party and Corridan's Xavier Institute of Industrial Relations] provided the only outlet for a frustrated rank and file.'[56]

The question of testifying in fact arrives somewhat late to the evolving script that became *On the Waterfront*. No doubt their own testifying is present somewhere in Schulberg and Kazan's minds. But the immediate cause may more likely be the weeks in late 1952 when a whole group of longshoremen testified against union leaders before the New York State Crime Commission. The opening of Arthur Miller's *The Crucible* on Broadway in January of 1953 to mixed reviews may have had its effect as well. Although Miller somewhat disingenuously denied that the play had any contemporary relevance, its seeming condemnation of informing through its tortured hero John Proctor made *The Crucible* into Miller's counterblast against anyone who had named names to HUAC. Not incidentally, despite the great success of *Death of a Salesman*, it had not been directed by Elia Kazan.

Arthur Miller in *The Crucible* was using the past to talk about the present. But *On the Waterfront* was responding directly to current events. Kazan, like Schulberg, was looking for a different kind of model. In November and December of 1952, Schulberg had spent some forty days attending the hearings of the New York State Crime Commission, and it is after this experience that the issue of testifying for the first time enters the script, initially with scenes in which Father Barry fights with his own conscience over persuading Luke, a black longshoreman with a family, to testify. Perhaps the most important and most revealing of the real longshoremen who testified was Tony Mike DeVincenzo, a former hiring boss who had been showing reporters around the waterfront crime scene since 1950, and who in May of 1953 wrote an article for *True* magazine called 'The Mob Said They'd Kill Me for My Story'.

Kazan for his part met DeVincenzo while he and Schulberg were doing their research in Hoboken. The longshoreman became Kazan's opening into the issues of the film, just as Longhi and Berenson had been for Miller, and Corridan and Brownie were for Schulberg – each guide casting the waterfront in his own terms. For Kazan, Tony Mike was the embodiment of what he wanted Terry to be and he later introduced him to Brando. Tony Mike had spent time on the side of the mob, began to resent their bullying and corruption, and had been ostracised and threatened for his testimony. His character in Kazan's eyes was a mixture of brutality and tenderness, of aggression and insecurity. 'I doubt that Budd was affected as personally as I was by the parallel of Tony Mike's story,' Kazan writes in his autobiography. 'This hour at Tony Mike's was the instant of final commitment, when I saw that, in the mysterious way of art, I was preparing a film about myself.' Here was another place where Schulberg, the Hollywood prince, and Kazan, the insecure immigrant, however fruitful their collaboration, parted ways.[57]

Fathers, Brothers and Battles

> So you got a brother. Well, let me tell you something, you got some
> other brothers and they're getting the short end while Johnny Friendly
> gets mustard on his face at the Polo Grounds.
>
> Father Barry to Terry Malloy

Family relations, real and symbolic, are always close to the surface in *On the Waterfront*, even when such details as the relation between Johnny Friendly and Terry (their mothers were cousins) get eliminated as the script changes. Like some version of the Group Theatre itself, everyone is related either actually or psychologically, while at the centre is Terry, struggling to belong, as Kazan characterised himself, pushing for acceptance in the face of feeling like an inveterate outsider.

In his notes on the scripts, Kazan also frequently invokes family and friends to explain what he's looking for. Edie Doyle, he observes, resembles his daughter Judy in her romantic view of the world, while in her mixture of self-righteousness and dependency she also resembles his wife Molly. When he emphasises that Terry has been brought up not to trust women, Kazan adds in parenthesis to himself 'cf also your uncles'.

Terry is also close to Schulberg. In an earlier draft, an Air Force veteran with a teenage son, Terry metamorphoses into a youthful ex-boxer later in the script's development and his changing characterisation clearly draws on Schulberg's own interests. In early scripts there are even scenes in which Terry takes Edie to a fight that he throws in order to show her what he does and how he can take punishment. This fascination with the boxer as a working-class figure whose prime resource is his body seems endemic in writers from the 1930s to the 1950s, with such landmarks as Clifford Odets's play *Golden Boy* (1937), Schulberg's own *The Harder They Fall* (1947) and A. J. Liebling's essay collection *The Sweet Science* (1958). Certain aspects of *On the Waterfront* do resemble the genre story of the down-and-out boxer who rallies for one last triumph, like Robert Ryan in *The Set-Up* (Robert Wise, 1949) or the late-blooming Sylvester Stallone in *Rocky* (1976), where the central motivation is always the battle for self-respect. Terry's pigeon-raising as well has its precedent in Schulberg's own hobby when as a teenager he was secretary of the Southern California Racing Pigeon Association.

But an immeasurable part of the central complexity of the film comes from the conflict between Kazan's basic belief that it is Terry's story and Schulberg's that it is Father Barry's. It is a delicate balance, a double focus, that ultimately seems to be resolved in Terry's favour but never dispenses with the controlling vision of Father Barry. He is the one who gets Terry to make that last walk down the pier, and it is his arm that Edie clutches in one of the last shots, as if to say, 'You were right after all.'

When Schulberg published his novel *Waterfront* a year after the film appears, he restored Father Barry to the centre of attention. We are privy to his inner life much more extensively than to that of any other character. Terry Malloy is much cruder, his relation to Edie Doyle (Katie in the novel) only hesitantly verges on the romantic, and he winds up as a corpse in a New Jersey swamp, never identified. Instead of gradually falling in love with him, Katie Doyle frequently feels total disdain.

But within the film Barry battles with Johnny Friendly for Terry's soul, the good father versus the bad father fighting over the wayward orphan – the contrast heightened by the down-trodden figure of Edie's father. Peter Biskind has argued that *On the Waterfront* tries to turn informing into 'a greater good' by 'the construction of sympathy: the creation of good guys and bad guys'. Visually, there definitely is some evocation of the urban darknesses of *The Informer* (1935), John Ford's film about the Irish rebellion. Ford was always a favourite of Kazan's, except this time it is the informer rather than the informed on who is cast as the martyr. But the question remains: how good is Father Barry and how bad is Johnny Friendly?

Kazan writes in his notes that the bond between Terry and Johnny must be a close and loving one. The early scene in which they wrestle good-naturedly in the bar has, notes Kazan, undertones that are 'close to homosexual between the two', almost a love scene. That homoerotic air seems totally in accord with Kazan's conception of their relationship:

Johnny Friendly pats Terry
on the face before he goes
to set up Joey Doyle: "You
take it from here, Slugger"

Johnny and Terry horsing
around in the bar

Terry trying to count the
take while Johnny touches
him affectionately and
Charley smiles

Johnny is the only person who has ever paid attention to Terry, who has ever indulged him and given him a place of warmth and acceptance. Terry loves Johnny, but at the same time feels a sense of shame at being the teacher's pet and mocked by the other mobsters. This troubled loyalty makes his final attack on Johnny all the more crucial, just as his love for his brother Charley finally founders on his realisation that Charley has been selling him out as well ('It was you, Charley, it was you'). As in Kazan's relation with Arthur Miller, which Miller calls 'brother-love', the tangle of love and disappointment between men is as strong, if not stronger, than any relation to women.

In this oedipal snarl a central behind-the-camera element is Kazan's relation to Brando. Brando had originally refused to do the script because of Kazan's betrayal of his Communist Party comrades and he felt it to be a personal betrayal as well by the man who had helped create his career. Brando's insistence that he be allowed to leave the set at 4.00 every day for his appointment with his psychiatrist is intriguing here as well, for who was Brando's psychiatrist? None other than Bela Mittelman, who had first been Molly Kazan's psychiatrist, then Kazan's as well. Kazan had recommended him to Brando when they were doing *A Streetcar Named Desire* together, and later believed that Mittelman might have been more instrumental than Spiegel in persuading Brando to sign on as Terry Malloy.[58]

Almost fifty years later, in an interview featured on the DVD, Rod Steiger is still hurt and angry about this. Not only did it seem to him that Brando was getting special treatment on a set that was supposedly more democratic than usual and by a director who was opposed to the star system, but it also undermined Steiger's desire to connect directly with the actor playing his brother. In fact, in the famous taxi scene, when we see Steiger in tight shots, he is often responding not to Brando off-screen, but to Kazan reading Brando's lines. Whether Kazan welcomed that atmosphere of professional betrayal as a way of injecting tension into the Terry–Charley relationship remains an open question.

Even more significantly, everything in earlier scripts that characterised Terry as sexually knowledgeable has been removed by the time of the final version. He hasn't been married before, he doesn't have a son, he doesn't come on to Edie sexually, and he doesn't banter with old conquests. Instead, as Kazan writes to Brando, there's 'something of the ascetic about him'.

Tempering Terry's essential loneliness, Charley, along with Johnny Friendly and the rest of the gang, have brought him up in a world of men without women, where D 'n D is the code and the credo is loyalty no matter what. Like the Irish Catholic working-class world of James T. Farrell's Studs Lonigan trilogy of the 1930s, the world of the Friendly gang is what Jonathan Yardley has called a 'macho cocoon'. Until the murder of Joey Doyle, it was a comfortable world for Terry, and he resists being pulled away from its solaces until his guilt becomes overwhelming ('Conscience … That stuff'll drive you nuts'). Kazan's notes keep emphasising 'photograph Terry's inner life', but in a sense the plot of the film is the creation of his inner life. Edie Doyle and his feelings for her are the vehicle of that change. But no matter how tenderly they finally kiss on the rooftop, the path to 'growing up' is never quite as simple as giving up the camaraderie of the boys for heterosexual love. In a broader sense, his own desire for tenderness has been repressed and ignored in his relation to the gang with its insistence on the tough-guy shield. Only with his pigeons can Terry indulge the feeling of innocence (and domesticity) otherwise missing from his life.

Tommy the Golden Warrior goes to meet Terry at the pigeon loft

Terry pensive after the murder of Joey Doyle

Later, when Edie comes to the roof, the Golden Warriors view her suspiciously

In the coop, Terry shows Edie his lead pigeon Swifty and makes a joke that leaves Tommy out

The longtime working title of *The Golden Warriors* indicates how much that other gang, with their logo-ed jackets and devotion to Terry makes the role of the mobsters more explicit. Johnny Friendly and his cronies are the Golden Warriors grown up. Unlike the jacket of Joey Doyle, which conveys the burden of responsibility and change, the Golden Warriors' jacket threatens to be as much a straitjacket as a suit of armour.

In earlier scripts, the Johnny Friendly character is a former Golden Warrior as well, but in the film Terry, the hero–boxer, is the progenitor of the group: 'I guess you could say I was the original Golden Warrior,' he jokes to Edie, as teenaged Tommy, 'my shadow', tussles with him. Tommy, played by Thomas Hanley, a non-professional actor who lived in the buildings where *On the Waterfront* was being filmed and who later became a hatch boss himself, is immediately hostilie to Edie. The intensity of Tommy's adolescent misogyny siphons off the lack of sympathy with women that is part of Terry's birthright. Women to Tommy represent weakness and Edie's presence on the roof can only arouse suspicion. What is this woman doing in his male space, with her ignorance of everything, including the lives of pigeons? 'She's beautiful,' says Edie, petting Terry's lead bird. 'She's a he,' sneers Tommy. 'His name is Swifty.' But then to Tommy's disgust Terry plays a joke and pretends to take an egg from under Swifty's belly. Terry and Edie grin, but not Tommy. Allegiances are shifting and he doesn't know why.

Father Barry also owes allegiance to a world of men without women, although some of his own moral stature, like Corridan's, comes from resisting the Church hierarchy's effort to play ball with the mobsters ('Don't blame me if they ship you off to Abyssinia'). But in contrast to this complex web of love, resentment and betrayal, Father Barry tends towards a moral rigidity that makes his commitment to social justice somewhat abstract. His most humanising trait is his constant cadging of cigarettes and Malden does a spectacular bit when, after sending Terry off to confess to Edie, he pulls a crumpled cigarette from his pocket that implies the actual anguish beneath his priestly assurance. Corridan was also a chainsmoker. Malden spent days with him studying his gestures and even went so far as to buy Corridan's long coat and hat to be more in character. But like Kazan's wife Molly, whom he called 'my Puritan', Father Barry, wrapped up in his own ideological interests, often ignores the contradictions in human nature and the human capacity for change as much as he does his own ideological interests. As Kazan remarks to Jeff Young, 'I don't like guys who are rigid and have one point

Barry's speech after Kayo Dugan's murder: "Some people think the crucifixion only took place on Calvary. They'd better wise up …"

"Boys, this is my church"

Barry after being pelted by the gangsters: "Christ is in the shape-up"

Barry gets a cigarette from Pop as they are hoisted out of the hold with Dugan's body

of view, who squeeze the complexities out of life.'[59] Barry is a more sympathetic figure than this, especially as Malden portrays him. But the single-mindedness and the angular rectitude are nevertheless there. In his letter to Brando, Kazan makes his own view clear: Father Barry never really likes Terry; he sees him as useful. The 'crucifixion' speech Barry makes in the hold after the death of 'Kayo' Dugan is an attack on greed and could easily be read as more anti-capitalist than anti-Communist. Like Corridan, Barry wants men to testify because it is their 'social responsibility'. What it does to their personal lives is not of as much interest until (in Schulberg's novel) he wrestles with the responsibility of sending people like Terry to their deaths.

Schulberg wants to see Terry as more physical than soulful, and this is the Terry that he recreates in his novel, where Father Barry's moral anguish is the centre of attention. The novel's Barry knows social theology and struggles with doubt, while its Terry is more akin to Lenny in John Steinbeck's *Of Mice and Men* or Meursault in Albert Camus's *The Stranger* – the inarticulate lower-class male who can express himself only in action. In short, Schulberg's Terry is Terry without Brando, without Brando's mixture of bravado and vulnerability, without the grace of his body, without his moody presence. Brando, like Burt Lancaster and Paul Newman, gives the lie to any theory of film that claims that its essence is the spectacle of the female body as gazed upon by men. In his first film *The Men* (Fred Zinnemann, 1950), in which he plays a paraplegic, it is the frailness of the male body that he must overcome. In *Streetcar* and *Zapata* it is frequently his unclothed torso that is the focus of attention. But in *On the Waterfront*, the spectacle of his body becomes an even more integral part of the plot because his character has been a boxer, a performer. 'When you weighed 168 pounds, you were beautiful,' says Charley to Terry in the taxi. Beautiful perhaps, but also a commodity, an object, as Edie rages at him in the bar scene: 'You say Johnny Friendly used to own a piece of you. I think he still does.' The reward for Terry's loyalty is to be treated like just another chunk of cargo. Again, it is Charley who makes the analogy: 'The girl and her father have their hooks in him so deep he doesn't know which end is up.'

As a boxer, Terry was the object of an audience's attention, and in never being allowed to be 'a contender', he is nobody.[60] Among the mobsters in their fancy overcoats and the longshoremen in their tattered work clothes, he seems to have no social identity of his own, just as he seems to have no place of rest but the roof. Small among the bulky tough guys, with milky smooth cheeks among the grizzled longshoremen, he fits as little visually as he will when he decides to turn against them.

Edie's apartment after Terry's confession: "I didn't say I didn't love you. I said stay away from me"

Embracing before the
flowered wallpaper in a
dim suggestion of a life
away from the waterfront

In essence, Schulberg appears attracted to Corridan/Barry as the representative of a Christianity that, unlike the Communist Party he had rejected, was sincerely a supporter of social justice and a moral channel for the working-class vitality of longshoremen like Brownie. This priest may be a member of a hierarchy threatened by corruption through worldly power, but he at least is still in touch with his own working-class roots and can compassionately live up to the ideals of his religion. Cast in this way, Corridan's anti-Communism doesn't find its way into *On the Waterfront* explicitly at all.

Kazan's radicalism, by contrast, while equally committed to social justice, seems by his own account derived more from an immigrant resentment of the rich and upper class, while at the same time being less urban and more agrarian in its primary allegiance, a politics exemplified in films like *Viva Zapata!* and *Wild River* (1960).

As film-makers both the scriptwriter and the director necessarily stress individual agency in making things happen, but Kazan's inner plot here and elsewhere in his films focuses more on the individual striking out to achieve or re-achieve a sense of personal dignity. His conclusions are less collective than Schulberg's, less concerned with social forces and social contexts, and finally more suspicious of the group and its motives. In contrast, Schulberg writes in his introduction to the novel *Waterfront*, Terry is 'a single strand in a rope of intertwining fibers', while 'the film's concentration on a single dominating character, brought close to the camera-eye, made it aesthetically inconvenient, if not impossible, to set Terry's story in its social and historical perspective.'

In the novel, unlike the film, many longshoremen testify, not just Terry. By wanting to supply the larger context for the waterfront story in his novel, Schulberg consciously or unconsciously seeks to right a balance that the film's focus on Terry and his emotions – as conveyed by Brando's performance – has upset. Schulberg's story is the intellectual emerging from isolation and engaging with the world, Kazan's the physical unreflective person who finds a conscience and love – an inner self. Kazan is attracted to the story of the scorned and even despised man who proves himself, Schulberg to the disengaged intellectual who has to realise that the world is hard but justice is still worth fighting for.

'We lost the battle, but we have a chance of winning the war'
These remarkably fruitful contradictions in the way Kazan and Schulberg see the main issues of the film come together without being resolved in the final scenes. Terry on the witness stand is an embarrassed

and inept figure, uncomfortably dressed up, and we see very little of his testimony. The main action is instead Johnny Friendly's blustering threats and Terry's defiant response. When he returns to the apartment building, trailed by a couple of sarcastic cops, he goes up to the roof, where he meets Edie and makes his decision to confront Johnny at the shape-up.

Here is the real climax, not the testimony. In line with the need for Terry to make his defiance a performance that vindicates all the dives he has taken in the past, the confrontation with Johnny Friendly, which in every previous script takes place in the union office, here occurs on a virtual stage before the eyes of all the longshoremen. Despite Edie's warnings, he takes Joey's jacket and decides to go down to the shape-up. He tells her he's going to 'get my rights', but this sounds like he's mouthing a phrase left over from the hearings. Once again, the political plot and the personal either collide or awkwardly overlay each other: Terry is after revenge.

Malcolm Johnson had called the waterfront a 'lawless frontier', an image of the old West that Leonard Bernstein slyly emphasises in his music by drawing directly on the 'Gun Battle' sequence of Aaron Copland's music for Lincoln Kirstein's ballet *Billy the Kid* (1938) for many of the violent scenes. Perhaps if Kazan had known this, he might not have thought Bernstein's music was so outlandishly operatic, since he also saw the film in part as a Western and might have warmed to Copland's music for the story of the innocent boy turned outlaw: 'It was a clear and elemental struggle. ... A lot of Westerns become mythic because they deal with fundamental moments and basic events.'[61] On the river, on the edge, will be the final confrontation.

In an earlier script, when the action was still inside the office, Kazan noted that Terry's speech could be cut, since it was making 'an irrelevant point'. Bringing it outside onto the gangplank in front of the longshoremen clearly changed the equation. 'I'm glad what I done to you,' says Terry, and Brando stretches out his arms and looks to his audience for a response. 'You done it to Joey, you done it to Dugan, and you done it to Charley, who was one of your own.' 'You talk yourself into the river,' says Johnny Friendly, and the fight begins. With the mobsters jumping in to help Johnny when it looks as if Terry is winning ('That boy's fightin' like he used to'), Terry is terribly beaten, his body lying practically in the river. As Father Barry and Edie rush to help him, dark blood gushes from his nose and mouth, suggesting severe internal injuries, and, when he's lifted to his feet, he doesn't even know if he's standing up.

Terry plays to the crowd of watching longshoremen

After he has almost beaten Johnny bloody, the gang almost kills Terry,

as the men watch silently: "He's one of theirs anyhow"

"The little rat's yours"

Terry lying half in the river

The longshoremen come to where Barry and Edie are helping Terry: "Terry walks in and we'll walk in with him." Another interesting example of Kazan's blocking

Barry whispering to Terry: "Johnny Friendly's layin odds that you won't get up"

"Am I on my feet?"

Terry stumbles up the gangplank while Barry stops anyone from helping him

Walking past the watching longshoremen, Terry clutches his broken ribs

The door starts to descend as the men walk in

Johnny Friendly, although bloody himself, still blusters in command. 'What about Terry?' shouts one of the men. 'He don't work, we don't work.' 'Work?' says Johnny contemptuously. 'He can't even walk,' and he starts pushing the longshoremen toward the pier. Then Pop Doyle finally uncorks his own anger and pushes Johnny into the river – a revolt that is easier for the watching group to get behind than Terry's. They laugh and chortle, and several run to the injured Terry to get him to lead them in.

Edie wants to leave him alone, until he can get help for his wounds. But for Father Barry this is the crucial moment. At first his appeal to Terry is abstract: 'You lost the battle, but you got a chance to win the war.' Terry doesn't respond. Then, his eyes darting from side to side, Barry pushes the button he knows Terry will respond to: 'Johnny Friendly is laying odds that you won't get up.' It's a line Kazan pencils into the script himself, the line that transforms Terry from a person into a symbol and, like the moment when Barry sends Terry down to confess to Edie, it makes the priest into a kind of director.

Barry zips Terry's jacket and Terry gets up, staggers up the gangplank, and almost falls. Edie tries to help him, but Barry pulls her back: 'Let him alone.' With the camera on his bleeding face and his staggering steps, Terry walks towards the open door of the pier. 'OK,' says the ship owner, 'let's get to work.' Terry goes in, followed by the men, while Johnny Friendly, pulled out of the river, threatens them. 'I'll remember every one of you.' Father Barry and Edie watch, and she clutches his arm as he looks down at her with a bemused smile. The door of the pier slams shut. The End.

I've gone into some detail about this last scene because it has aroused so much controversy. Terry has realised how much he has been manipulated by Johnny Friendly and his brother Charley, but has he actually become autonomous? What has his body-breaking gesture of taking this emblematic walk actually solved? In earlier scripts, which often included the arrest of Johnny Friendly by Edie's policeman Uncle Frank, there were stage directions about triumphant liner whistles and Irish rebellion folksongs on the soundtrack. But here the triumph, if triumph it be, is much more melancholic, as Bernstein's music emphasises.

Perhaps Father Barry has it backwards: the battle has been won, but not the war. Mr Big and the higher-ups who run Johnny Friendly have been virtually removed from the film, except for the scene, which Schulberg says he fought to include, of the rich man turning off his set

"Mr. Upstairs" watches the hearing on television

Johnny Friendly tells Terry, "You just dug your own grave. You're dead on this waterfront"

Johnny tries to stop the longshoremen from following Terry in, as Barry and Edie watch in the background

after Terry's testimony and telling his butler that he will no longer accept calls from Johnny Friendly.[62] When I spoke to Schulberg about the film, he made only two critical comments about Kazan's direction, both in the final scene. One was that he wanted Johnny Friendly's threats to be delivered in a tighter (and therefore more intimidating) shot, while Kazan's overhead shot of Johnny amid the crowd of longshoremen ignoring him as they follow Terry minimises his power. The other was the shot of Edie clutching Father Barry's arm. 'Their friend has been beaten to a bloody pulp and they're smiling?'[63]

In fact, even as the film was being shot, the kind of results that Father Corridan and the insurgent longshoremen expected as a result of the exposure of waterfront and union corruption were not coming to pass. In September 1953 the ILA had been expelled from the American Federation of Labor (AFL) for corruption, and in November, when *On the Waterfront* was beginning principal photography, Joseph P. Ryan was forced to retire after he had been indicted for bribery. But just before Christmas, and a month before the production wound down, the ILA had won an election against the new waterfront union set up by the AFL. In May 1954 the new union lost again. Some reforms were later put into place, including the outlawing of the shape-up. But the people in power essentially remained the same, and Corridan himself was removed from his post at the Xavier Institute of Industrial Relations and sent by the Church to teach economics in Syracuse.

All the tensions in the final scene – between Kazan's emphasis on the individual gesture and Schulberg's on the group revolt, between Kazan's focus on Terry's reclaiming of his sense of dignity and Schulberg's on Barry's effort to inculcate a moral conscience – are thus only exacerbated by the relation of the film to the conflicts in the real waterfront world out of which it had grown. Terry may galvanise the longshoremen, but does he or can he actually lead them to victory? Lindsay Anderson characterises them as 'leaderless sheep in search of a new master'. But, even after being beaten, Terry does not really engage their sympathy. Until he makes his walk, they sit silently watching ('he's one of theirs anyhow'). Finally, bloodily, he has separated himself from both the gang and the other longshoremen. Neither a leader nor a martyr, he is instead a symbolic rallying cry. And the 'real' Terry – who knows? In most Hollywood films that engage in any way with politics, the ending is usually a romantic resolution. The forces of history are too large to be resolved neatly, and the only way to end the film is with an embrace. But here the embrace, such as it is, is not between the hero and the heroine, but between the heroine and the priest. Finally the film is both open-ended (Will Johnny Friendly's threats come true? Will Terry continue to prevail? Will he and Edie find lasting love?) and closed. 'Let's go to work,' says the fat cat ship owner, and the iron door comes down on the longshoremen, not much of a happy portent for the future. Like the last-second escape that Edie and Terry make from the truck about to run them down (a scene Kazan added to the script), is this also a victory that could easily have turned into a defeat?

Lindsay Anderson calls the ending 'implicitly (if unconsciously) Fascist', meaning that the audience has been manipulated into accepting the political message by 'hysterical film-making' that uses 'every possible device to batter and bemuse'.[64] But the varieties of manipulation are exactly the subject of the film. The question of who is the sincere and who the insincere manipulator crystallises the ambivalence that infuses the final scene, a doubleness akin to Kazan's own directorial and autobiographical stance as both manipulator and victim of manipulation. Is political radicalism, communism with a small 'c', either the way to a good society or to freedom of the individual, and what happens when those two imperatives conflict? Schulberg and Kazan, each with his own agenda and his own doppelgänger in the story, nowhere more than here display their own uncertainties – through performances that themselves, as Kazan insists, are built upon contradictions that make the characters human.

After the Waterfront

But instead of the film falling apart under the burden of its own contradictions, it has remained powerful, perhaps in part because of them. No one would care much about its meaning if the film itself hadn't retained its grip on the imagination, and so the urge to give the elements of *On the Waterfront* some unified explanation also remains strong. Sometimes it seems to me that critics who insist on reading Kazan and Schulberg's testimony as the essential meaning of the film feel too lured by the film's emotional force and want to distance its rich inconsistencies by a single-noted clarity. On the other hand, there are those critics who push the political themes away and dwell instead on the aesthetic side of the film, especially the acting. But *On the Waterfront* is a complex experience larger than either of these limited perspectives.

Some of the people who helped make the film have similarly tried to recast the story in their own coherent voices. Kazan, throughout many interviews, both enthusiastically accepts and rejects his identification with Terry Malloy. Although at one point in the scriptwriting process he marginally notes that Terry's defiant speech ('I'm glad what I done to you'), is repetitious and should be cut, in his autobiography he writes 'that was me saying with identical heat, that I was glad I testified as I did'. Later, in his book-length interview with Jeff Young, he seems to take it back. '... I never meant any parallel between Terry and me because the issue in the film is terribly clear.'[65]

Schulberg, always more engaged with the details of the waterfront struggle, feels even more strongly that making any parallel between the testifyings 'marginalizes what the longshoremen actually did when they had to testify, under threat of being killed. The whole thrust of that story is lost if you think it's just about HUAC.' But his subsequent writing of more journalistic pieces about both the waterfront and the film, his novel, and then, almost thirty-five years later, his play version all indicate his own urge to rewrite and reshape the film.

Leonard Bernstein as well, while praising the film, felt disgruntled about how his own contribution was treated. In a short essay entitled 'Interlude: Upper Dubbing, Calif.' he expresses awe for the ability of the sound mixer even as he has to keep reminding himself that the music is

> really the *least* important part, that a spoken line covered by music is a line lost, and by that much a loss to the picture, while a bar of music completely obliterated by speech is only a bar of music lost and *not* necessarily a loss to the picture.

Finally, writes Bernstein, a composer, after watching his carefully constructed notes cut and eliminated, has to accept, 'be it with a heavy heart, the inevitable loss of a good part of his score', to see what he is doing 'not as a composer but as a man of the theatre'.[66] Accordingly, a little more than a year later, Bernstein writes his *On the Waterfront* suite to restore all those notes dropped in Upper Dubbing.

Before the film was released there was a lively correspondence between Sam Spiegel's office and Joseph Breen of the Production Code office, which begins with Breen asking for a Catholic technical advisor to consult on the character of Father Barry, and then goes on to list various complaints about excessive brutality, vulgarity in language and sexual suggestiveness. Aside from restaging the scene of Terry at Edie's apartment to eliminate them being on a bed when they embrace, the most interesting aspect of this negotiation over what to censor and what not is the moment when Charley says 'What the hell' in the taxi scene. Now covered over on the soundtrack by the honk of a car's horn, this is sacrificed, perhaps with some premeditation, to the bar scene in which Terry tells Barry twice 'You go to hell' before Barry slugs him. Breen is so convinced this is an appropriate compromise that he writes to Eric Johnston, the head of the Motion Picture Association, that he wants the Board to make a specific exception in this case because the phrase is 'used seriously and with intrinsic validity'.

When the film surprisingly opened to great critical and financial success, other issues came out of the woodwork. Monticello Films sued Schulberg, saying that they still owned the rights to the script, and lost. Frank Sinatra sued Sam Spiegel for reneging on his casting, got a court order to check Spiegel's books, and the case was settled out of court. Tony Mike DeVincenzo also sued, for $1,000,000, saying that Terry Malloy's story paralleled events in his own life. After Brando testified that

Kazan had told him to study Tony Mike as a model, the suit was settled for $25,000.[67]

The shape-up has been gone for many decades, much of New Jersey shipping has moved away from Hoboken, and today's longshoreman is more likely to run a computer or crane than swing a hook. Although northern New Jersey locals say that the now-containerised waterfront is still influenced by some of the old gangs, who have been romanticised in such shows as *The Sopranos*, not much of the world of *On the Waterfront* remains in its old form. Hoboken has become gentrified, and boasts many restaurants that have made their way into laudatory articles in the *New York Times* Food section. River Street is now graced, if that's the word, with high-rise apartments and gentrified shops.

But the myths of the film and the world it created have only flourished. The bar where Terry and Edie had their first drink and dance together is now called Frankie and Johnny's On the Waterfront café. Down the street, there's a Hoboken Historical Museum which recently featured an *On the Waterfront* exhibit. Although the narrow, dank apartments and the pigeon coops are long gone, walking tours of the locations were available during the celebrations of the fiftieth anniversary of the film in May 2004. Karl Malden says he doesn't remember the slapping by Kazan during the bar scene that so amused the extras gathered at Pepe's when I visited in the late 1960s, although he does say that when tough little Tommy weeps and says 'A pigeon for a pigeon', it was probably Kazan who slapped him enough to get the tears going. Thomas Hanley, who showed up for the celebration, said he was crying because he was scared by a 'bad cop' who locked him in a room.

But beyond the myths the allure of the film and its hypnotic ambiguities remains. Is it Kazan's film? Is it Schulberg's? Is it Brando's, or Saint's, or Malden's or Steiger's, or Cobb's, or Boris Kaufman's, or Bernstein's …? The list, if not quite endless, certainly includes many people, all of whom contributed their part to its final effect. How then to sort out the factors that make *On the Waterfront* great, without making them all fit together?

Schulberg has often written against the auteur theory and championed the crucial role of the writer in making a film, even while he acknowledges the importance of his working relationship with Kazan, to which the numerous revisions of the script, covered with Kazan's handwriting bears mute testimony. So many of Kazan's choices move the script away from the verbal to the visual, but at the same time the lines in the script and the racing energy of its plot carry us inexorably forward. It was an intense atmosphere that inspired the actors as well. As Eva Marie Saint has said, the set was closed, with only occasionally tolerated visitors. There was no time for talking on the phone to family, friends, or agents. Everything was focused on the film and people stayed in character. Then the production was over and they went their separate ways. I asked her if there were any retakes. Yes, she said, she was called back a few weeks later for some insert close-ups, but they were never used. 'In the meantime my husband and I had gone skiing. I had gotten a little tan, my cheeks were pink. I wasn't Edie anymore.'

NOTES

· ·

1 This and later quotations from Kazan's notes come from the Eila Kazan Archive at the Wesleyan University Cinema Archive, Wesleyan College, Middletown, Connecticut. They are cited here by courtesy of the Archive.
2 Miller, *Timebends*, p. 147. Panto's body was actually found in a lime pit in New Jersey in January 1941. See Turkus, pp. 410–13; Mello, pp. 5–6; Kimeldorf, pp. 124–5.
3 The title refers to the setting in the Red Hook area (hook=spit of land) as well as to the traditional longshoreman's hook for loading cargo.
4 Kazan, *A Life*, p. 412.
5 Miller, *Timebends*, p. 308; Kazan, *A Life*, p. 415.
6 Indirectly Kazan was later told that, if he went forward with another waterfront script, he would never direct another Miller play, although he never knew whether Miller himself knew of the threat *A Life*, (p. 508). With no evidence, Gottfried speculates that the two had made a deal that if Kazan wouldn't name Miller, Miller wouldn't sue or impede Kazan from making a waterfront film (Gottfried, *Arthur Miller*, p. 235).
7 Schulberg's earlier versions are in the library of Dartmouth College. Copies, with Kazan's notes and other material, are in the Kazan Archive at Wesleyan University. The script published by Schulberg is the shooting script rather than the script of the final film, and interesting comparisons can be made between the two. Kazan says in his autobiography that he cut 'large chunks' during filming. Eva Marie Saint's script at the Library of the Motion Picture Academy of Arts and Sciences has her own annotations of lines that were cut.
8 Coincidentally, Curtis (1920–88) had been attached to First Army Headquarters during the war as a court stenographer and assisted at the Nuremberg trials, although he and Schulberg never met there. He later was Josh Logan's assistant and frequent dialogue director for many years.
9 'I thought I had left filmwriting forever. After the war I hated the way writers were treated.' All quotations not otherwise cited from printed or archival sources are from interviews

conducted in 2004 with Schulberg, Eva Marie Saint, Karl Malden, Judy Kazan and Nick Kazan.
10 It was also referred to as the Xavier Labor School.
11 Corridan, who was dubbed the 'waterfront priest' by the newspapers, originally told Schulberg, 'We're doing tough stuff down here and don't need a Hollywood movie.'
12 *New York Times*, 7 January 1951.
13 On 8 January 1951, Kazan wires Zanuck that he and Miller will be arriving the next Monday to discuss *The Hook*. On 17 January 1951, the *New York Times* article reports that Schulberg and Siodmak, the director are already working on their script.
14 Epstein, 'None Without Sin', interview with Jim Longhi.
15 There are a few glimpses of Terry's apartment in earlier versions of the script and at first he even has a son.
16 Abe (Kid Twist) Reles, the Murder, Inc. informant who told of Panto's murder, said that the murderers specifically wanted to destroy the body to deprive the rebel longshoremen of a martyr. 'It was well known that Panto had no enemies except the mobsters. … Thus, it would be best if the corpse never turned up' (Turkus, p. 411).
17 Kazan, *A Life*, p. 524. Parts of Corridan's original speech are printed in Johnson, pp. 222–3.
18 Schulberg had once researched their trial for a book on lynching (*Moving Pictures*, pp. 420–1).
19 The ad is reproduced in Bentley, *Thirty Years of Treason*, p. 484. Kazan says his wife wrote it in *A Life*, p. 464.
20 But compare Schulberg's *Cosmopolitan* article of March 1954, 'The Terror of a Water-front Wife', where he quotes Helen 'Dolly' Mullins, whose brother had testified to the Crime Commission: 'Is it ratting when you do what Eddie did, the truth in order to get the mob off your backs?' Whereupon Schulberg writes, 'At this point I couldn't resist telling Dolly that the film I had been working on for the past year with director Elia Kazan … was based on exactly that issue.'

21 Kazan discusses the character in his *Saturday Review* letter, 5 March 1952.

22 Kazan, *A Life*, p. 480.

23 Kazan, *A Life*, p. 488.

24 Schulberg, Afterword to *On the Waterfront* script, p. 147.

25 I've checked through the *Hollywood Reporter*, *Variety* and *Daily Variety* for this period and haven't been able to find the reference.

26 Behlmer, *Memo from Darryl F. Zanuck*, p. 230.

27 Says Ingo Preminger, 'The blacklist opened the way for Sam to hire top writing talent for little money' (Fraser-Cavassoni, *Sam Spiegel*, p. 115). Until 1943 Spiegel's first business partner had been Boris Morros, who later wrote *My Ten Years as a Counterspy* (1959) about his activities as a Soviet spy from 1937 to 1947 and then as a double agent.

28 *Hollywood Reporter*, 25 May 1953.

29 Garfield died of a heart attack in May 1952.

30 Sinatra was to be paid $55,000 plus one per cent of the net profits. He later sued for breach of contract. See below, footnote 67. Sinatra later often proclaimed his belief that Brando was the 'most over-rated actor in the world' and referred to him as 'Mumbles', But he admired Lee J. Cobb's performance in *On the Waterfront* and in 1955 came to Cobb's aid after the actor suffered a massive heart attack, helping to pay his hospital bills and other expenses (Kelley, *His Way*, p. 225).

31 According to Fraser-Cavassoni, Spiegel's biographer, Joanne Woodward had also been considered for the role of Edie. Spiegel had offered the script to Jennifer Jones and Grace Kelly, with how much seriousness it's hard to gauge, since such star personalities would hardly fit the film's effort at psychological authenticity. Karl Malden recalls Kazan's request that he rehearse both Saint and Elizabeth Montgomery for the role before Saint was finally chosen (Malden, p. 240).

32 Schulberg's rage against Spiegel makes a good story and Kazan repeats it, but something may be askew in the chronology, since in a script in Kazan's files dated 'circa 4/1/53' all the cutaways and reaction shots are already there.

33 Personal conversation.

34 Kaufman had begun making films in the Paris of the 1920s with Jean Vigo and later worked with Herbert Grierson in Canada. Like other members of the cast and crew, he was to go on working with Kazan in later films as well (*Baby Doll*, *Splendor in the Grass*, etc.).

35 Because the script published by Schulberg is the shooting script rather than a transcript of the final film, in this book I will quote from the film.

36 The meeting is held in the lower church of Sts Peter and Paul, which faces on Stevens Park. Terry and Edie emerge from the façade of Our Lady of Grace ('OLG', as Pepe called it) into Church Square Park at 4th and Willow. Then that park merges into Elysian Park at 10th and Hudson with the river view.

37 This scene was added by Kazan. In Schulberg's shooting script, Charley doesn't give Terry the gun in the taxi scene. Terry gets it out of a pawn-shop window after finding Charley's body, cutting his hand in the process.

38 Kazan also mentions Cartier-Bresson's photograph of a funeral procession as inspiration for the first scene.

39 Young, *Kazan*, pp. 30, 36.

40 Intriguingly, Albert Maltz, another blacklisted writer, wrote the script for *The Robe*. Ben Barzman, also blacklisted, worked on the scripts of both *Give Us This Day* and *He Who Must Die*. So much for 'godless communism'?

41 On Kazan's religion, see Ciment, *Kazan on Kazan*, p. 112. See also Young, *Kazan*, p. 191: 'I'm not in anyone's stream. I really don't like any sort of establishment, right, left or whatever, where you are to think what people expect you to think.'

42 See Murphy, p. 24, quoting Esther Jackson, 'a subordinate system of plastic symbols'.

43 Brando, *Songs My Mother Taught Me*, p. 206.

44 A more prominent character in Schulberg's script than he is in the film, Mutt wanders in and out of the action. In the script, but not in the film, he is present on the street when Terry calls Joey to come up to the roof.

45 Kazan, *A Life*, pp. 525–6.

46 Kazan, *A Life*, p. 429. See also the
comments on Kazan's directorial style by Barry
Primus in Lawrence, *Dance with Demons*,
p. 307.
47 Young, *Kazan*, p. 162.
48 This whistling is unaccountably erased
from the soundtrack of the 2001 Columbia
Special Edition DVD. According to Grover
Crisp at Sony, it was actually on the music track
rather than the dialogue, that is, it was added in
post-production. This is plausible since, when
the film wrapped, Bernstein had yet to write the
music. The DVD also uses an incorrect aspect
ratio. The original, says Crisp, was probably
1.85 rather than 1.33.
49 I suspect it must have been Spiegel's idea,
another effort to raise the prestige of the film.
Howe refers to the helicopter shot in letters to
his wife, 25 and 27 March 1954 (Herrick
Library).
50 Young, *Kazan*, p. 57.
51 Miller, 'Arthur Miller Ad-Libs on Elia
Kazan', *Show*, 1964, in *Conversations*, pp. 70–1.
52 Brando, *Songs My Mother Taught Me*,
p. 195.
53 Navasky, *Naming Names*, pp. 209–10.
54 The labour historian Colin J. Davis
describes a typical occasion: 'Ryan responded
to the meeting with his usual barrage of anti-
Communist rhetoric' (p. 103). Davis also
remarks that Corridan wanted 'to create a cadre
of activists that could confront and challenge
both the corrupt ILA leaders and Communist
militants' (p. 144) but his 'bitter feelings toward
Communists at times clouded his judgment ...'
(*Waterfront Revolts*, p. 151).
55 Father Corridan goes to talk to McCormack
in April 1952 to try to persuade him to make
concessions to the longshoremen. In 1945, a
grand jury had criticised O'Dwyer for not
pursuing legal action in the death of Abe Reles.
In 1941 Reles had fallen out of the window of
his supposedly protected hotel room shortly
before he was to testify for O'Dwyer against
Albert Anastasia in a series of murders
including that of Pete Panto. This was the
occasion when mob boss Lucky Luciano
supposedly said, 'He could sing but he couldn't
fly' – a line that one of Johnny Friendly's

mobsters uses after the death of Joey Doyle.
56 Davis, *Waterfront Revolts*, p. 141.
57 Kazan, *A Life*, p. 500.
58 Kazan, *A Life*, p. 516. While visiting New
York, Alfred Kinsey took sexual histories from
the entire *Streetcar* cast and crew.
59 Young, *Kazan*, p. 50.
60 A contender in boxing lingo is specifically a
fighter who can respectably fight with an actual
champion. In other words, all Terry wants to
have done is aspire.
61 Young, *Kazan*, p. 172.
62 Leta Schlosser, who grew up in Hoboken
and whose father Dudley Austin Schlosser was
involved in the movement to reform city
government there, tells me that Mr Big is played
by Richard Marnell, Sr, who was cast for his
resemblance to 'Big Bill' McCormack.
63 Lindsay Anderson also objects to this:

> For all her fragile appearance, there is the
> spirit of a Spartan mother within the breast
> of Edie; seeing her lover disappear, battered
> almost out of recognition and hardly able to
> stand, to perform a day's labour in the
> dockyard – she smiles contentedly' (p. 128).

The possibility also remains that in fact this is a
reaction shot when they overhear two new
mobsters saying that now they'll have to
actually go to work. That's a moment that exists
in virtually all the scripts, but not in the final
shooting script or the film.
64 'The Last Sequence of *On the Waterfront*',
p. 130.
65 Kazan, *A Life*, p. 500; Young, *Kazan*, p. 179.
66 Bernstein, pp. 67, 69.
67 A *Hollywood Reporter* item (26 March 1956)
says that Sinatra was suing for $500,000.
According to Spiegel, Sinatra wanted $100,000,
but settled for $18,000. Kitty Kelley, citing an
interview with Spiegel, says that 'He and
Spiegel settled the lawsuit amicably, without
any exchange of money' (p. 228).

CREDITS

· ·

On the Waterfront

USA
1954

Directed by
Elia Kazan
Produced by
Sam Spiegel
Screenplay by
Budd Schulberg
Based upon an original story
by Budd Schulberg
Suggested by articles by
Malcolm Johnson
Director of Photography
Boris Kaufman
Film Editor
Gene Milford
Art Director
Richard Day
Music by
Leonard Bernstein

© Columbia Pictures
Corporation
Production Company
Columbia Pictures
Corporation presents
an Elia Kazan production
a Horizon picture

Production Manager
George Justin
Assistant to Producer
Sam Rheiner
Assistant Director
Charles H. Maguire
Dialogue Supervisor
Guy Thomajan
Script Supervisor
Roberta Hodes
Wardrobe Supervision
Anna Hill Johnstone
Wardrobe Mistress
Flo Transfield
Make-up Supervision
Fred Ryle
Hair Stylist
Mary Roche
[Title Design
Dale Tate]
Sound
James Shields

Cast
Marlon Brando
Terry Malloy
Karl Malden
Father Barry
Lee J. Cobb
Michael J. 'Johnny Friendly'
Skelly
Rod Steiger
Charles 'Charley the Gent'
Malloy
Pat Henning
Timothy J. 'Kayo' Dugan
Leif Erickson
Inspector Glover
James Westerfield
Big Mac
Tony Galento
Lewis P. 'Truck' Janotta
Tami Mauriello
Tillio A. Rodelli
John Hamilton
'Pop' Doyle
John Heldabrand
Mutt

Rudy Bond
Moose
Don Blackman
Luke
Arthur Keegan
Jimmy Collins
Abe Simon
Barney
Eva Marie Saint
Edie Doyle

[uncredited]
Anne Hegira
Mrs Collins
Thomas Hanley
Tommy Collins
Michael V. Gazzo
waiter at Johnny's bar
Barry Macollum
J. P., Johnny's banker
Fred Gwynne
Mladen 'Slim' Sekulovich
Mike O'Dowd
Daniel D. 'Specs' Coogan
Martin Balsam
Gillette
Robert Downing
Father Vincent
Pat Hingle
waiter

Nehemiah Persoff
taxi driver
Dan Bergin
Sidney, the butler
Rebecca Sands
police stenographer
John Finnegan
Joey Doyle
Lee Oma
Johnny Friendly's bartender
Richard Marnell, Sr
Mr Upstairs
Sidney Armas
longshoreman
Matty Russo
longshoreman
Joe Luciglini
Marlon Brando's standin
Tiger Joe Marsh
Pete King
Neil Hines
3 cops in court struggling
with Johnny
Johnny Seven
longshoreman
Joyce Lear
Jere Delaney
Donnell O'Brien
Clifton James
Vincent Barbi
Lilian Herlein

9,676 feet
107 minutes and
32 seconds

Black and White
MPAA: 12916

Credits compiled by
Markku Salmi

ACKNOWLEDGMENTS

In any collective enterprise, especially the collision and collaboration of talents that is film-making, it is possible to consider the final product to be the creation of luck and accident more than premeditation and design. That the result should be a great work only compounds the irony. In a similar way, many people were extremely supportive in helping me gather the material for this book and many happenstance remarks and fragments of conversations over the years about *On the Waterfront* found their way into its making. Let me mention a few important contributions here.

Eva Marie Saint, Karl Malden and Budd Schulberg gave freely of their time to discuss the film with me, as did Nick Kazan and Judy Kazan. John Finnegan, who played Joey Doyle, spoke to me from his home in Palm Springs about having to lie dead on the freezing ground of Hoboken for seven takes and more. Thanks to Geoff Cowan, Howard Rodman, Miles Beller and Kristine McKenna for their help in making some of these interviews possible.

Jeff Young generously shared with me his own ideas about the film as well as some of the material he had developed in his own interviews with Kazan which formed the basis of his book *Kazan: The Master Director Discusses His Films*.

At Wesleyan University, Leith Johnson and Joan Miller made available the fascinating archives of Elia Kazan's career housed there. Barbara Hall at the Motion Picture Arts and Sciences Library (which Karl Malden helped found when he was president of the Academy), opened its tremendous resources in Hollywood history. Grover Crisp, the head of the film restoration department at Sony, showed me a beautifully restored print of the film before its release and kindly filled me in about some of the technical issues in its production. Christopher Harter of the Lilly Library, University of Indiana, allowed me access to the script of Arthur Miller's *The Hook*. Eileen Lynch at the Hoboken Historical Museum gave up a rainy Sunday afternoon to show me around the exhibit with its many fascinating memorabilia of the film collected from local residents.

Leta Schlosser was filled with fascinating information about growing up in Hoboken during the time the film was being made. Nick Beck pointed me to the wide range of Budd Schulberg's journalistic work before, during and after the filming.

For help in tracking down the facts about the life and murder of Pete Panto, my thanks to Nunzio Pernicone and Dorothy Gallagher.

Thanks as well to Lou and Jim Antonio, for their memories of the Actors Studio in the 1950s; to Christina Pickles, for her reminiscences about the impact of *On the Waterfront* on a group of fledgling British actors; and to William Baer, for helping me decide which role was played by the former boxer Lee Oma.

I first saw *On the Waterfront* when I was a teenager and I could not put down in such a narrow space the almost innumerable conversations I had with friends then and since about the film, nor those I had with students when I later came to teach it in a course on the 1950s that itself has been going on for thirty years.

But a few in particular I would like to mention here: Michel Ciment, Larry Goldstein, Leonard Orr, John Romano, Kenny Turan and especially, Peter Biskind, with whom I've argued about the film for years, and Richard Schickel, my West Coast colleague in Kazan studies.

Finally, my deep gratitude to those who read the manuscript and enhanced it by their insight: Dorothy Braudy, David Freeman, Dana Polan, Marita Sturken (also a fine Hoboken informant) and Rob White, my editor at the BFI.

SOURCES

· ·

Allen, Raymond, *Waterfront Priest*, intro. Budd Schulberg (New York: Henry Holt, 1955).

Anderson, Lindsay, 'The Last Sequence of *On the Waterfront*', *Sight and Sound*, January–March 1955, pp. 127–30.

Barrett, James R., *William Z. Foster and the Tragedy of American Radicalism* (Urbana: University of Illinois Press, 1999).

Beck, Nicholas, *Budd Schulberg: A Bio-Biography* (Lanham, MD: Scarecrow Press, 2001).

——, Budd Schulberg: An Exhibition in Observance of the 50th Anniversary of the Publication of *What Makes Sammy Run?*, 4–29 March 1991. Doheny Library, University of Southern California.

Behlmer, Rudy (ed.), *Memo from Darryl F. Zanuck: The Golden Years at Twentieth Century-Fox* (New York: Grove Press, 1993).

Bell, Daniel, 'The Racket-Ridden Longshoremen: The Web of Economics and Politics', in *The End of Ideology: On the Exhaustion of Political Ideas in the Fifties* (New York: Free Press, 1962).

Bentley, Eric (ed.), *Thirty Years of Treason: Excerpts from Hearings before the House Committee on Un-American Activities, 1938–1968* (New York: Viking Press, 1971).

Bernstein, Leonard, 'Interlude: Upper Dubbing, Calif.', *The Joy of Music* (New York: Simon & Schuster, 1949, pp. 65–8).

——, *On the Waterfront*: Symphonic Suite', in *Bernstein Century: Bernstein*, conducted by Leonard Bernstein (Sony Classical SMK 63085).

Brando, Marlon, with Robert Lindsey, *Brando: Songs My Mother Taught Me* (New York: Random House, 1994).

Ciment, Michel, *Kazan on Kazan* (New York: Viking Press, 1974).

Copland, Aaron, *Billy the Kid*, in *Bernstein Century: Copland*, conducted by Leonard Bernstein (Sony Classical SMK 63082).

Davis, Colin J., *Waterfront Revolts: New York and London Dockworkers, 1946–61* (Urbana: University of Illinois Press, 2003).

DeVincenzo, Tony Mike, 'The Mob Said They'd Kill Me for My Story', *True* (May 1953), pp. 18–27, 101–7.

Epstein, Michael, 'None Without Sin: Arthur Miller, Elia Kazan and the Blacklist' (written and directed by Epstein), *American Masters*, PBS, 2003.

Fraser-Cavassoni, Natasha, *Sam Spiegel* (New York: Simon & Schuster, 2003).

Freeman, Joshua B, *Working-Class New York: Life and Labor Since World War II* (New York: New Press, 2000).

Gottfried, Martin, *Arthur Miller: His Life and Works* (Cambridge, MA: Da Capo, 2003).

Hirsch, Foster, *A Method to Their Madness: The History of the Actors Studio* (New York: W. W. Norton, 1984; Da Capo, 2002).

Hurley, Fr. Neil, S. J. '"On the Waterfront": Blending Fact and Fiction Not Always Successful – But Worked in This Instance', *Daily Variety*, 28 October 1988.

Johnson, Malcolm, *Crime on the Labor Front* (New York: McGraw-Hill, 1950).

Kazan, Elia, *A Life* (New York: Knopf, 1988).

Kelley, Kitty, *His Way: The Unauthorized Biography of Frank Sinatra* (New York: Bantam, 1986).

Kimeldorf, Howard, *Reds or Rackets? The Making of Radical and Conservative Unions on the Waterfront* (Berkeley: University of California Press, 1988).

Lawrence, Greg, *Dance with Demons: The Life of Jerome Robbins* (New York: G. P. Putnam's Sons, 2001).

Logan, Joshua, *Josh, My Up and Down, In and Out Life* (New York: Delacorte, 1976).

——, *Movie Stars, Real People, and Me* (New York: Delacorte, 1978).

Malden, Karl, with Carla Malden, *When Do I Start? A Memoir* (New York: Proscenium, 1997).

Manso, Peter, *Brando* (New York: Hyperion, 1994).

Mello, William, 'The Legacy of Pete Panto and the Brooklyn Rank-and-File Committee', *Italian American Review*, forthcoming.

Miller, Arthur, 'Arthur Miller Ad-Libs on Elia Kazan', in Matthew C. Roudané (ed.), *Conversations with Arthur Miller* (Jackson: University Press of Mississippi, 1987).

———, *Collected Plays* (New York: Viking, 1957).

———, *Timebends: A Life* (New York: Grove Press, 1987).

Murphy, Brenda, *Tennessee Williams and Elia Kazan: A Collaboration in the Theatre* (Cambridge: Cambridge University Press, 1992).

Naremore, James, *Acting in the Cinema* (Berkeley: University of California Press, 1988).

Navasky, Victor S., *Naming Names*, 3rd edn (New York: Hill and Wang, 2003).

Peyser, Joan, *Bernstein: A Biography*, revised and updated (New York: Billboard Books, 1998; New York: Beechtree Books, 1987).

Reppetto, Thomas, *American Mafia: A History of Its Rise to Power* (New York: Henry Holt, 2004).

Robinson, Paul, *Bernstein* (New York: Vanguard, 1982).

Schickel, Richard, *Brando: A Life in Our Times* (New York: Atheneum, 1991).

Schulberg, Budd, 'How One Pier Got Rid of the Mob', *New York Times Magazine*, 27 September 1953.

———, 'Joe Docks, Forgotten Man of the Waterfront', *New York Times Magazine*, 28 December 1952.

———, *Moving Pictures: Memoirs of a Hollywood Prince* (New York: Stein and Day, 1981).

———, *On the Waterfront: The Final Shooting Script* (Carbondale: Southern Illinois Press, 1980).

———, 'The Terror of a Waterfront Wife', *Cosmopolitan*, March 1954, pp. 82–91.

———, *Waterfront* (New York: Donald I. Fine, 1955).

———, with Stan Silverman, *On the Waterfront: The Play* (Chicago: Ivan R. Dee, 2001).

———, 'Waterfront Priest', *Commonweal*, 3 April 1953, pp. 643–6.

Schwartz, Nancy Lynn, *The Hollywood Writers' Wars* (New York: Knopf, 1982).

Sinclair, Andrew, *Spiegel: The Man Behind the Pictures* (Boston, MA: Little, Brown, 1987).

Smith, Wendy, *Real Life Drama: The Group Theatre and America, 1931–1940* (New York: Knopf, 1990).

Turkus, Burton B. and Sid Feder, *Murder, Inc.* (New York: Farrar, Straus & Giroux, 1951).

Vineberg, Steve, *Method Actors: Three Generations of an American Acting Style* (New York: Schirmer, 1991).

Wertheim, Albert, '*A View from the Bridge*', in Christopher Bigsby (ed.), *The Cambridge Companion to Arthur Miller* (Cambridge: Cambridge University Press, 1997), pp. 101–14.

Young, Jeff, *Kazan: The Master Director Discusses His Films* (New York: Newmarket Press, 1999).

ALSO PUBLISHED

If you would like further information about future BFI Film Classics or about other books on film, media and popular culture from BFI Publishing, please write to:

BFI Film Classics
BFI Publishing
21 Stephen Street
London W1T 1LN

**BFI Film Classics '... could scarcely be
improved upon ... informative, intelligent,
jargon-free companions.'**
The Observer

Each book in the BFI Publishing Film Classics series honours a
great film from the history of world cinema. With new titles
published each year, the series is rapidly building into a collection
representing some of the best writing on film. If you would like to
receive further information about future Film Classics or about
other books on film, media and popular culture from BFI
Publishing, please fill in your name and address and return this
card to the BFI.* (No stamp required if posted in the UK,
Channel Islands, or Isle of Man.)

NAME

ADDRESS

POSTCODE

E-MAIL ADDRESS:

WHICH *BFI FILM CLASSIC* DID YOU BUY?

* In North America and Asia (except India),
please return your card to:
University of California Press, Web Department,
2120 Berkeley Way, Berkeley, CA 94720, USA

BFI Publishing
21 Stephen Street
FREEPOST 7
LONDON
W1E 4AN